HEIRESS

By the same author

HRH Princess Margaret:
A Life Unfulfilled

Nigel Dempster

HEIRESS

— The Story of —

CHRISTINA ONASSIS

GROVE WEIDENFELD

NEW YORK

Published by Grove Weidenfeld
A division of Wheatland Corporation
841 Broadway
New York, NY 10003-4793

First published in Great Britain in 1989 by
George Weidenfeld & Nicolson Limited.

Library of Congress Cataloging-in-Publication Data

Dempster, Nigel.
    Heiress : the story of Christina Onassis / Nigel Dempster. —1st
ed.
        p. cm.
    ISBN 1-55584-384-0
    1. Onassis, Christina.   2. Greece—Biography.   3. Celebrities—
Greece—Biography.   4. Upper classes—Greece—Biography.
I. Title.
CT1118.053D46   1990
949.507'092—dc20
[B]   89-23281
                                                                 CIP

Manufactured in the United States of America

Printed on acid-free paper

First Edition 1989

1 3 5 7 9 10 8 6 4 2

Acknowledgements

I am indebted to the cooperation and frankness of a great number of people involved in this story who went out of their way to assist me. Including those who generously contributed to Peter Evans's original research for *Ari*, almost four hundred people were contacted in preparation for this book. For a variety of personal and professional reasons, many of them asked not to be mentioned by name. I thank them all.

To none am I more indebted than to Luis Sosa Basualdo, and Alberto and Marina Dodero in Buenos Aires; the Marquess of Blandford in London; Florence Grinda in Paris; Jean-Noël Grinda in Gstaad; and Reinaldo Herrera in New York. Without their candid, detailed reminiscences of their long, close and diverse relationships with Christina, this book would have been infinitely less explicit, and far less well informed. They were among the closest and oldest friends Christina had, and without their help, counsel and, above all, their invaluable indiscretions, I would not have been able to present the intimate, and, I trust, true picture of the heiress that appears in the following pages.

Among the many journalists and writers I owe thanks to are my *Daily Mail* colleagues John Edwards, and William Lowther in Washington; Dudley Freeman and his excellent New York News Service; the late Sam White in Paris; Sabine de Labrosse and Jean-Pierre de Lucovich of *Paris-Match*; Anthony Haden Guest; John Miller; Brian Wells; and Taki Theodoracopulos.

I am indebted to Anthony Montague Browne for finding time in his busy schedule to give me his impressions of Christina as a small child; Jane Hoare-Temple for sharing with me her memories of playing as a child with the heiress aboard the yacht *Christina*, and also for letting me read her diary entries for Easter 1961 spent with the Onassis family in the West Indies; to Lady Sargent, for kindly searching her photograph albums for pictures of the young Christina; and Lady Carolyn Townshend. The contribution of Hélène Gaillet has been so significant that she deserves a page to herself, as does Christophe Gollut. I finally thank Mercedes Zavalia, whose closeness to Christina in the last days of her life gave her important insights to the heiress's state of mind at that time, for the interviews she gave me during my visit to Buenos Aires in February 1989.

Peter Evans

It is my good fortune that my friend Peter Evans did not want to write another Onassis book after *Ari,* his best-selling biography of Aristotle Socrates Onassis. Instead he persuaded me to embark on this biography of Christina. He not only encouraged me every step of the way but also gave me hundreds of pages of his notes and transcripts gathered originally for his own book. These included hours of intimate and revealing conversations with Ari, with the young Christina herself, and with the friends, relations and plain hangers-on who surround the very rich. This exciting and unique material, together with his pages of explanations, insights, suggestions and answers to my unending questions and demands on his experience, I have used shamelessly throughout these pages. Indeed, every word in this book has in one way or another been influenced by him. He declined my suggestion that a more proper credit should be: Nigel Dempster and Peter Evans. But only that could convey the measure of my feelings about his contribution to this book. The absence of his name on the cover in no way diminishes the debt and gratitude I feel.

N.D.

Contents

Illustrations

Christina is baptized in New York (Frank Spooner/GAMMA)
Alexander and Christina with grandfather Stavros Livanos (Frank
    Spooner/GAMMA)
The Onassises land in Nice, 1955 (Rex Features/SIPA)
Christina, aged seven, with her mother (Rex Features/SIPA)
Maria Callas with Ari (Press Association)
Tina Livanos Onassis marries the Marquess of Blandford (Popperfoto)
Ari and his *Chryso mou*, and Alexander (*Daily Mail*)
Alexander and Christina at Ari's wedding on Skorpios, 1968 (Rex
    Features/SIPA)
Baroness Fiona Thyssen-Bornemisza and Alexander (Rex
    Features/SIPA)
Christina and Ari (Rex Features/SIPA)
Danny Marentette (Danny Marentette)
Luis Sosa Basualdo and Christina (Alpha)
Luis Sosa Basualdo, 'Gaucho' (Luis Sosa Basualdo)
Basualdo and Christina at the Corviglia Club, 1971 (Luis Sosa Basualdo)
Twenty-year-old Thierry Roussel with Christina (Frank
    Spooner/GAMMA)
Mick Flick and Christina (Pictorial Parade)
Christina with Florence Grinda (Rex Features/SIPA)
Peter Goulandris and Christina (Camera Press)
Joseph Bolker and Christina (Rex Features/SIPA)
Christina with Ari near the end of his life (Rex Features/SIPA)
Christina and Jackie Onassis leaving the American Hospital in Paris
    (Popperfoto)
Christina with Philippe Niarchos (Rex Features/SIPA)

—1—

All heiresses are beautiful

John Dryden
King Arthur

ON 10 OCTOBER, 1988, A MONDAY, Christina Onassis remained in bed most of the day in her fifth-floor boudoir on Avenue Foch, the sound of the Paris traffic muted by the thick walls and the armour-glazed windows hung with heavy blue drapes. A compulsive telephone caller, she rang no one; an incorrigible gossip, she would take no calls. Only her beloved Eleni, who had looked after her for almost as long as she could remember, and understood her better than anyone else alive – only Eleni knew what day it was.

The fourteenth anniversary of her mother's death – a day, Christina said, that would always be sad and always be dear to her; although, in truth, they had never been close in life. But as usual, she had taken it hard. There were those, she knew, including Stavros Niarchos – a man who was both her uncle and her stepfather – who believed that she had caused her mother's death.

As it had so many times before, the anniversary had turned Christina's mind to thoughts of her own mortality, to wills, and to her only child Athina's future. The feeling that time was running out for her was in her mind on that unhappy anniversary. In two months' time she would be thirty-eight years old. 'My mother was only six years older than I am now when she died,' she told a friend that evening in Paris, 'and I used to think of her as being positively *middle-aged*.'

Thierry Roussel, her fourth and former husband, the father of Athina, and a man she still obsessively loved, had been pleading with her all that summer to make changes in her will which he felt did not adequately take care of their child, who was now three months short of her fourth birthday. He urged her again and again to remember that Athina's inheritance 'will be in your hands ... stretching out to her from heaven'. It would be a double tragedy, he would worry aloud with paternal practicality, if something were to happen to Christina before her hands were properly poised. Christina knew that he was right, and only the gloriously busy summer itself – and some uncertainty about how to redistribute her wealth, which she privately estimated in excess of $500 million – had caused the delay.

But on that second Monday in October, 1988, she finally made arrangements to fly to Switzerland for a meeting with her ex-husband, her lawyers and financial advisors, to change her will for the ninth and last time since her father, the legendary billionaire Aristotle Socrates Onassis, died in 1975. In the evening she called Rudi Metzler, the pilot of her Falcon 50 jet, to file a flight plan to Geneva for Wednesday morning, 12 October. She then drew up a list of the beneficiaries who were to be sacrificed in order that she could give more to Athina – and, for the first time, include Athina's father – in the last will and testament of Christina Onassis.

It was, she would tell a friend in Buenos Aires, *'une nuit blanche –* the hardest night of my life'. Out went her uncle George Livanos, her mother's younger brother and himself a millionaire; out went her aunt Kaliroi, her father's half-sister, who had lived well on Onassis largesse, but had no fortune of her own. Longtime business associates were dropped, old friends who had once been given expectations became unremembered.

Two days later, Christina sat in the Geneva office which dealt with all her legal affairs and on plain foolscap paper began writing with her 22-carat gold broad-nibbed Parker Duofold pen:

MY WILL

I, the undersigned Christina Onassis, daughter of Aristotle Onassis and Athina Livanos, being of age and enjoying fully my physical and mental capacities, hereby make my last will and testament and state that in the event of my death, I wish and direct that my estate (including my inheritance from my father and my mother) be distributed to the following beneficiaries, in the proportions and the amounts stated opposite the name of each one of them to the exclusion of all other relatives and any other persons.

Alone in a small under-furnished interview room, for more than an hour she wrote – in her neat, upright, schoolgirl hand – from her prepared notes. The finished document, in English, was five pages long. Seven beneficiaries ('the magnificent seven', she called them wryly) were to share $6.6 million; Thierry Roussel was to receive a life annuity of $1.42 million provided that the annual income produced from the estate for Athina was not less than $4.25 million. Everything else 'of any kind and description whatever, real or personal, tangible or intagible [sic] ... I leave and bequeath to my beloved daughter Athina to be hers absolutely...' Her affairs were to be 'managed prudently and diligently' until her eighteenth birthday by a board of four Greeks and Thierry Roussel. A simple majority vote would decide all issues.

––––

Exactly one week later, Aerolineas Argentinas flight AR121 began its journey from Paris to Buenos Aires. Beside Christina Onassis in the second row of the first-class cabin was her personal interior decorator and *copain* Atalanta de Castellane, *née* Politis; in front sat Eleni Syros. Dark and attractive and looking ten years younger than her 'fifty-three summers', as Christina called them, Eleni was more than a maid and companion: she took care of everything – clothes, jewellery, passports, tickets, and, most vitally, the Gucci holdall containing the many elixirs so indispensable to Christina's capricious sense of well-being.

Except for a single Amytal capsule to help Christina sleep, Eleni had no recourse to the Gucci's contents, even though the flight had been delayed by a nerve-jangling six hours in Paris. Once the 747 was airborne on its thirteen-hour journey, Christina, who was addressed as Madame Roussel, the name on the passenger list, relaxed almost completely. She refused the offers of vintage champagne, asking for Coca-Cola. On a diet – she had recently shed forty pounds in a Swiss clinic and was determined to lose another twenty – she declined the choice of entrées for dinner, passed on the Iranian Beluga caviar. She nibbled on canapés and hors d'oeuvres. Showing no interest in the in-flight movie, she gossiped for hours with Atalanta before finally taking the Amytal.

Christina was flying to Buenos Aires to attend the fortieth birthday party of her friend Marina Dodero. She would be staying four days. It did not seem unreasonable to her to travel 6,900 miles in nineteen hours ($15,570 just for the tickets) for one party, a visit of a few days. Once she flew from Paris to London to make a single direct-dial telephone call to a lover in Moscow. Another time she took the Concorde flight from London to New York for a *cing-à-sept* with a movie star, and returned the same evening. 'Now that *was* a quickie,' she liked to end that particular story. It was, she believed, what jet-setting was all about.

Marina, and her husband Alberto, with two unmistakable bodyguards in tow, were waiting at the airport to greet *La Reina*, the Doderos' pet name for Christina. (Marina, who first met the Onassis heiress fourteen years earlier, when she was Marina Tchomlekdjoglou, the daughter of Greek expatriate owners of a large textile business in Argentina, also regarded Christina as her spiritual 'little sister'.)

It was spring in Argentina, the sky a very pale blue. During the sixty-minute drive from the Aeropuerto Internacional de Ezeiza to the city, Marina revealed that Christina had been booked into the Alvear Palace, rather than into the better-known Plaza Hotel, which had long been regarded as the Onassis hotel in Buenos Aires; the Alvear Palace, in the smart Recoleta residential district, was only one hundred and fifty yards from the Dodero apartment on the Avenue Callao, and thought to be more convenient for Christina's short visit. Privately, Christina was not pleased with the arrangement, although she did brighten up a little when she was told that she had been given the most luxurious of the forty apartments in the hotel: suite 602 on the sixth floor.

Mercedes Zavalia, in charge of the hotel's customer relations, and aware of the publicity value of having the world's most famous heiress under her roof, nervously detected Christina's less than enthusiastic mood when she arrived. She hoped it was simply travel-tiredness. Mercedes was more concerned to see the two heavies accompanying the party. The instructions she had received clearly stated that the visit was to be strictly low-key. Her experience told her that bodyguards and moderation was an unstable mix. In addition to which, she had made no arrangements for bodyguards. In fact, she had heard that although Christina was fanatical about guarding her daughter (two British ex-commandos stayed with her day and night), she frequently eschewed protection for herself. Mercedes quietly conveyed her worries to Marina Dodero. 'Clutterbuck,' murmured Marina, cryptically referring to a local businessman whose recent kidnapping had put fear into the rich families of Buenos Aires. 'I fear for my own safety, and for Dode's,' she said, using her husband's nickname. 'The bodyguards are for us.'

In her suite, Christina settled down with a glass of Coke (the frigibar had been stocked with two dozen cans) and began dialling her friends around the world. Still unpacking the cases and putting the jewellery (including a diamond drop valued at $2 million) into the room safe, Eleni could hear her mistress becoming increasingly irritated by the incompetence of the world's telephone systems in general and by having to use her index finger to dial in particular; Argentina had yet to catch up with the push-button telephone, which Christina believed was an absolute necessity in a civilized world. Eleni paid no attention to the loud grumblings and oaths coming from the sitting room; it was not new to her that people could behave like this: thirty years before she had performed the same role for Maria Callas, and had become immune to the *malheurs* of the rich and famous.

But the Argentine telephone company and Christina Onassis continued to be incompatible and finally she summoned Mercedes Zavalia's help. The public relations director handled the crisis with the immediacy that bespeaks the style of an old pro. Within minutes, Thierry Roussel was on the line from Geneva. 'And all was right with the world again,' recalled Mercedes, who was briefly to become close to the troubled guest, and already knew the story of her continuing love for her former husband, a man considered to be a considerable cad by many of Christina's friends.

But, indeed, it seemed to be Roussel's louche and sensual ways with women that had given him such a powerful and lasting fascination for Christina. ('Thierry is a Frenchman,' she once sought to excuse his chauvinism towards her. 'He thinks it's better to hide behind his vices than to show off his niceness.') Part of Roussel's allure sprang from his air of inherent privilege and class which none of her previous husbands – a Los Angeleno, a Muscovite, a fellow Greek – could equal in her frankly starry eyes. Unfortunately for his besotted bride, Thierry Roussel also possessed an extreme sense of independence. And six months after the birth of Athina, he also had a son, Erik – by his unforsaken Swedish mistress, Gaby Landhage. The disclosure of Roussel's double life was both a private shock and a public humiliation to the richest girl in the world – but she forgave him, as she always would, and now made light of the infidelity, calling it the Malmo Conspiracy, after the name of the town in Sweden where Gaby gave birth to his son.

Now speaking French, her second language after English, in which

Roussel was less than fluent, she began their daily ritual rap. 'Christina called it her "fix"; she never tried to hide her need to hear Thierry's voice, even when they had little that was new to say to each other they would talk every day for at least a couple of hours,' said a Paris friend who knew the routine.

After she had spoken to Roussel, Christina called her own Paris number and talked to her daughter in their private mixture of English and French, bright chatter about delayed flights, hotels, the shopping she planned to do in Buenos Aires – 'a woman's town', she thought, perhaps because it was filled with the reassuring names: Christian Dior, Yves St Laurent, Emmanual Ungaro, Ralph Lauren, even Harrods – investing in the child a maturity beyond her years. She told Athina about the Café la Biela, where, on her first visit to Argentina sixteen years before, she had caused such a fuss when she left her purse containing $20,000 on a table, and forgot to report its loss to the police. ('That was very silly, Mummy,' Christina would later proudly tell friends was Athina's reaction to the story.) At 5 p.m. she called room service and ordered a salad, which she ate while continuing to call her friends across the world. There was no urgency to her day. She had bought Marina's birthday present in Paris (an emerald ring set in diamonds). Her only appointment – with Andrea, the hairdresser – was not until five o'clock the following afternoon. Slowly, surely, Christina Onassis was winding down.

Marina Dodero's fortieth birthday party at Le Club on Friday, 21 October, turned out to be one of Buenos Aires' social spectaculars of 1988. The guests said so, the press said so, and even those who weren't invited suspected that it was true. But Marina's big four-oh counted for nothing in the order of billing that night: Christina was the star. The band struck up the theme from *Zorba the Greek* as soon as she appeared, dressed in Ungaro black, and from that moment on she was the centre of attention. As the evening wore on, she would become an object of speculation, too.

At the buffet dinner, she sat with Marina's brother Jorge Tchomlekdjoglou, whom she had known for almost as long, but not nearly as well, as she had known Marina. For while Marina and Alberto had spent vacations with Christina in St Moritz, Paris, and on Skorpios, her private island in the Aegean, Jorge had dutifully continued to run the family textile business in Argentina (in which Christina had invested $4 million in 1981, when receivership beckoned). So while there was the warmth of a long relationship between Jorge and Christina, there was also an element of exploration which gave the evening a special frisson.

Fat or thin, Christina loved to dance. She would take to the floor and dance for hours. She would dance with men, with women, with complete strangers sometimes. She could dance with Greek abandon; she could move with tangoesque sensuality. But only with husbands and lovers would she dance close when the music became slow, only with them would she close her eyes. She was never self-conscious on the dance floor.

Jorge tried to keep up with her that night, but Christina made it quite plain that it was she who was monopolizing him. A bachelor (his late mother, to whom he had been close, 'was the only woman in his life,' according to *alta sociedad* gossip), two years older than Marina, Jorge was not used to so much attention from a woman.

It is difficult to imagine exactly what was on Christina's mind. But she had not enjoyed herself so much for a very long time, she said. Instead of her usual Coca-Cola, she drank champagne. She left the party at 5 a.m. She seemed very happy and rather drunk.

At the hotel, Eleni was waiting up to undress her, to put her into a fresh nightgown; to see she took the right pills, to put her to bed, and to talk, if that was what Christina wanted, until the heiress fell asleep.

———

Christina's hangover was apparently mild enough for her to be ready almost on time to leave the following day for the Doderos' rented house in the grounds of the Tortugas Country Club, twenty-five miles northwest of the city.

It was a perfect day, the temperature nudging seventy degrees Fahrenheit. They took the Pan American Highway. Christina sat in the back of the limousine, between Eleni and Atalanta de Castellane. Alberto and Marina sat in the front, pointing out the interesting places en route, the famous Palermo Polo Fields, the Hippodrome racecourse, and gossiping about the wonderful party. But nobody mentioned what they all suspected – that telephones were ringing across the pampas with the hottest new rumour: 'Jorge could be *el nuevo* – the fifth Mr Christina Onassis.'

As they neared the Tortugas house, Alberto warned Christina not to expect too much in the way of luxury. Their new home there would not be ready to move into until 1 December, and they had been lucky to be able to rent anything, he said. But there were plenty of compensations, he assured her: 'Any sport you want is there – swimming, tennis, golf, polo, horseback riding.'

Christina touched her forehead with the palm of her hand. 'I think I'll pass on the exercise today, thank you, gang,' she said.

They all laughed.

Christina felt comfortable with these friends, she was at home in their world. And even her accommodation, a single bed in a small room, a single rail on which to hang her clothes, amazingly did nothing to alter her mind.

During the evening she explored with the Doderos and Jorge the possibility of spending time, perhaps an annual season – spring seemed perfect – in Argentina. Her questions were direct: how much were apartments? Were apartments a better investment than houses? What was safest? Perhaps an *estancia* outside the city would be best? She grew excited (as did Atalanta, who had made a great deal of money decorating and redecorating Christina's many homes) and regretted having to leave again for France the next day.

'Why Argentina?' asked a friend in Paris, for whom that country had no appeal at all.

'Fate exists,' Christina had answered.

—2—

The days before we just had to
sign for whatever we desired

Christina Onassis

CHRISTINA BELIEVED IN OMENS, and Buenos Aires was the city where, sixty-five years before, her father had started *his* new life, and made the first million of the Onassis fortune. It was a fact the Argentinians never let her forget, and the reason why they regarded her as a superstar – their superstar – a *porteña*, as the dwellers of the port city called themselves.

Her father had been on her mind a great deal during that summer. She had acquired a video of the ABC television miniseries based on Peter Evans's biography *Ari*. And although she had been unable to bring herself to read the book – 'I'm afraid of what I might discover in it,' she told friends – she repeatedly watched the Hollywood drama, retitled *The Richest Man in the World*.

Christina had always identified with her father. She never identified with her pretty, English-educated mother, Athina (who had wanted her aborted, and barely hid her disappointment with her daughter's looks). Christina had a dark complexion, her hair was black and harsh, her eyebrows thick. She resembled her father like no one else, and the story of his early struggles in Buenos Aires now touched her profoundly.

She, who most of her life had expressed almost no interest in her family history – 'A point is the beginning of all geometry; a percentage point is the beginning of all fortunes,' Aristotle Onassis had stonewalled when Christina asked about his early years: 'Before that point nothing matters' – suddenly began to display an inordinate fascination in what she jokingly but accurately sometimes called 'the days before we just had to sign for whatever we desired.'

9

You had to go back a long way to find such days. You had to go back to the beginning of the century.

———

Aristotle Onassis's father, Socrates, a small, short-necked man with a sunbaked Levantine face and dark sceptical eyes, was a Turkish citizen with a Greek soul, and the richer he got the more Greek he became; it was *chic* to be Greek, the Greek writer and socialite Taki Theodoracopulos would later remark. But born and brought up deep in the interior of Asia Minor in a village called Moutalasski, Turkish would always be his first and only comfortable language. In the 1890s, after the railroads had opened up the great wealth of the Ottoman Empire to the West, he heard of the rich pickings to be made in Smyrna. Tobacco, cotton, timber, carpets, coal, barley and figs were pouring through the port every minute of every day. Socrates and his brothers Homer, Alexander and Basil took off to make their fortunes.

Grandfather Socrates worked hard, harder than any of his brothers, and within two years he had saved enough money from his clerk's wages to rent a small warehouse and open an import–export agency handling whatever goods he could turn around at a profit. He gained a reputation for his shrewdness as well as for the quality of his goods. Inside a year he moved into larger premises on the Grand Vizier Hane in the centre of the business quarter. He mortgaged part of the warehouse to the Imperial Ottoman Bank to get cash to insure cargoes and finance caravans.

As his fortune grew and his reputation rose, Socrates acquired a villa in Karatass, a cosmopolitan, middle-class suburb a ferry ride from the city. And just as it was his village-mindedness more than his stinginess that caused his move to the suburbs, so it was tradition rather than romance that took him back to Moutalasski to propose to Penelope Dologlou, the daughter of a village elder.

Eleven months after they were wed in St Paraskevis's church in Smyrna, just seven weeks before her seventeenth birthday, Penelope developed labour pains. The doctor from Smyrna failed to arrive on time and a neighbouring Armenian housewife was summoned to help with the delivery. Penelope gave birth to a daughter, whom they baptized Artemis.

Aristotle Socrates Onassis was born, probably, although by no means positively – for he would alter the day, the month and the year to suit his purpose – two years later, on the morning of 20 January 1900. Uncle Alexander, who was given the honour of being the first to hold his brother's first-born son, declared that the infant was a typical Onassis; Penelope, on the other hand, believed she saw her mother in the boy's brown eyes and sensed a special destiny in him too, telling her husband: 'He will cast a long shadow, this one.'

It had been a difficult birth; Penelope never had another child. Although she suffered constant poor health, the next dozen years were pleasantly enriching ones for the Onassis family.

Unlike his brothers, Socrates had stayed clear of politics. Politics was for fools. There had been a bloody uprising in Constantinople. Sultan Abdul Hamid had been deposed by the Young Turks, who brought in an ominous policy of Turkey for the Turks. In 1909 hundreds of Armenians were massacred at Adana. A chill of apprehension ran through the Christian population. Socrates quarrelled bitterly with his brothers for joining the Asia Minor Defence League, an organization demanding autonomous Greek territories inside Turkey, with Smyrna – because of its large Greek population – treated as an international zone.

But in 1912, it was tragedy on a smaller scale that struck the Onassis family. After what was thought to have been a successful operation to remove an abscess in her kidney, Penelope died.

Little Aristotle, who would feel the loss of his mother's love well into his manhood years, and talk of her with emotion long after he became a parent himself, came under the influence of his paternal grandmother, Gethsemane. An unwavering Christian who believed in heaven and hell, retribution and eternal damnation, Gethsemane prayed each night that her grandson would grow up to be a priest; devotional to the point of unbalance, every week she sent his underclothes to be blessed at the church where he served as an altar boy and learned the Byzantine psalms by heart.

Less than six months after Penelope's death, Socrates married again. He wanted more sons. He wanted heirs growing up to take over the tobacco business which was now the major Onassis interest. His second wife, Eleni, produced two daughters, Merope and Kaliroi, but no more sons. Aristo, who had grown into a small, thin child with a misleading look of vulnerability, became alarmingly mollycoddled in the female-dominated household.

In later years, Onassis enjoyed telling how it was uncle Alexander who saved him from becoming 'a complete namby-pamby' – or, if grandmother Gethsemane had had her way, 'a creeping Jesus'. More significantly, according to Peter Evans, uncle Alexander inculcated in his nephew 'the power of charm, and also perhaps the charms of power. He put into his head ideas and concepts that would shape his whole life. Ideas about passion and revenge, dark Greek concepts of loyalty and love, and an ancestral sense of defiance that Aristotle Onassis would never shake.'

Encouraged by uncle Alexander, Aristotle became a keen competitive sportsman: he swam, rowed, played water polo for the Pellos sports club. Although small, he was proud of his physique, and enjoyed showing off in front of girls. Scion of a prominent family in Smyrna society, he knew he had all that was needed to be successful – connections, charm, and cash. (Cash, according to headmaster Michael Avramides's testimony recorded for the Athens Centre for Asia Minor Studies in 1961, frequently embezzled from the school servants' funds.)

Socrates showed little interest in his son's academic progress. 'Great scholars are seldom rich,' he would say, fearful that too much education would fill his son's head 'with ideas above business'. As part of his apprenticeship, every evening he made Aristotle spend two hours in his office, getting acquainted with the atmosphere of business, and acquiring a respect for facts. 'Make a note of everything,' he told his son, 'especially people. If you meet them again, you will at once know how much time you need give them, how much attention they're worth.' Aristotle bought a notebook and began writing down his impressions, and his secrets. It was a habit he never lost. One day a long way in the future Christina would inherit the book.

In 1914, Turkey entered the world war on the side of Germany. The Moslem Turks took the opportunity to turn on the Christian minorities with a vengeance. There were wholesale massacres; churches were burned to the ground; Aristotle and his friends at Evangheliki, the best school in Smyrna, whose first language was English, were ordered to destroy their caps and wear fezzes and armbands displaying the Turkish star and crescent.

When the Armistice was signed in 1918, President Woodrow Wilson and Prime Minister David Lloyd George, largely to thwart Italy's territorial ambitions, supported the Greek occupation of Smyrna. The dangers of permitting Greek troops to occupy a city with such an hysterical culture were wilfully ignored.

Nevertheless, for the next two years Smyrna prospered under the Greek administration. Failing to graduate from Evangheliki, Aristotle went to work in his father's office on the Grand Vizier Hane. And in the whorehouses of Demiri Yolu he soon became a valued client. He did not mind that the girls did it for money, he told Evans. 'One way or another, sweets, that's the way all women do it,' he recalled one of the girls telling him. 'If you understand that you'll still get took, but you'll always know how you're took.'

In the summer of 1922, Smyrna fell back into the hands of Kemal Pasha's Turkish Nationalist Army. It was a brutal return. Moslem mobs ran through the streets murdering infidels; the Armenian quarter was set ablaze. Still Socrates insisted they personally had nothing to fear. He had kept clear of politics; he had many good Turkish friends. He was sure that unless you were a troublemaker you could go on leading your own life under the new regime, exempt from the worst oppressions.

His confidence was misplaced. Arrested and falsely charged with making payments to a Greek compatriot organization during the foreign occupation, he was taken to a concentration camp to await trial. Aristotle's stepmother and sisters were deported to the island of Lesbos, from where they were to be transported to mainland Greece. Aristotle's smallness and youthful good looks made it possible to claim that he was only sixteen. (Had he admitted to being any older, he would have been dispatched to the interior to work in a labour gang: 'And that was as good as a death sentence.') The Onassis villa had been commandeered by a Turkish general whose aide-de-camp permitted him to stay on as his unofficial batman.

Aristotle's friendship with the Turkish lieutenant became both close and intimate and he used it well. He acquired a military pass which got him into the prison camp to visit his father. Expecting to be executed at any moment, Socrates urged his son to contact a Turkish friend who had borrowed a large sum of money and given him the deeds to several houses as security. Socrates told Aristotle to offer to cancel the debt and return the deeds to the Turk if he would agree to organize a 'Turks for Onassis' petition. A few days later, several hundred signatures were presented to the governor by a deputation of 'concerned Turkish businessmen'. Socrates was moved out of death row; but he was not released.

Searching for the deeds hidden in his father's warehouse, Aristotle had also retrieved a large bundle of Turkish banknotes. With the help of a friendly American vice-consul (the family had always understood the value of contacts; this one had been cultivated by uncle Alexander) he decided to take the family savings and get out of the country as quickly as possible. The vice-consul arranged for him to leave on a United States destroyer which was due to sail for Lesbos the next morning.

The little island was glutted with refugees. Aristotle walked for days, leaden-souled, exhausted and hungry, searching for Eleni and his sisters. He caught up with them at last in a small camp at the foot of the Hill of Olympus – his stepmother, three sisters, aunts and cousins: seventeen scared women and children. (If the Onassis family was a tiny detail in the national trauma that followed the Smyrna holocaust, its loss was great. Three of Aristotle's uncles, including his beloved Alexander, were hanged; an aunt, Maria, together with her husband, Chrysostomos Konialidis, and their daughter, died when the Turks torched a church in Thyatira in which five hundred Christians were seeking sanctuary. Split up from Eleni and the girls, Gethsemane made it on her own to Greece, only to be knocked down and killed by a purse thief at the docks.) Determined to keep the family together, Aristotle bought deck space for everyone on a freighter bound for Piraeus. There was no joy in his heart, only sadness, as ten days after his twenty-third birthday he walked on Greek soil for the first time.

In Athens he was reunited with his father's last surviving brother. A vain, mean-minded man who now considered himself the head of the family, uncle Homer became indignant when Aristotle insisted that he had earned the right to be treated as an equal, and even pooh-poohed his nephew's achievement in getting the women and children safely to Athens. Aristotle retaliated by refusing to hand over the family savings; he would pay the bills and control the finances himself. There were bitter rows, but the bitterest were over the question of how to get Socrates out of prison. Homer wanted to hire lawyers, to go through the legal channels; Aristotle preferred to put his faith and his money into bribes – *mordiditas*, as he would later call them, the 'little bites' on which corrupt officials grow fat.

Eventually, Aristotle grew tired of arguing. He took off for Constantinople, then the capital of Turkey. Who he paid in that city is not known, but six weeks later his father was safe in Athens. Instead of gratitude, encouraged by Homer, the old man grilled his son about the money removed from the safe in Smyrna. Aristotle accounted for every penny – boat passages, food, rent, greasing official palms in Lesbos and Athens, and, the biggest sum by far, the cost of freeing Socrates himself.

Still there were distasteful suggestions of prodigality, and worse. A sense of injustice hung over Aristotle. He refused when Socrates offered him a job with the tobacco company he was planning to open in Athens. He had decided to emigrate. The United States was his first choice, but scrupulous immigrantion quotas had recently been introduced, and immigrants from Turkey were at the top of the unwanted list. His next choice was Buenos Aires, where he had distant relatives.

In August, 1923, with $250 in his pocket, travelling on a Nansen permit valid for a one-way trip for refugees going to a country of resettlement, he began his incredible journey.

––––––

Some of these stories Christina had heard before from her aunt Artemis, who remembered so well the Smyrna years and the way things had been; seeing them recreated on television, watching the portrait of her father as a young man (played by Raoul Julia), the violent ups and downs of his life, profoundly moved her, yet did not alter her high spirits as she contemplated her own new beginning in Buenos Aires. 'I never really understood how much he had done in his life,' she told Hélène Gaillet, a New York friend of her father's, who had asked what she thought of the ABC series. 'He should have talked to me more – I would have understood him a whole lot better if he had been more open with me,' she said.

Buenos Aires in 1923 was not the Buenos Aires Christina knew in 1988. Poor as his daughter would never be poor, hungry as she could never believe, Aristotle Onassis was one of the thousands of refugees from the eastern rim of Europe – Syrians, Armenians, Lebanese – scornfully lumped together as *Turkos*. He went through the gamut of menial jobs – dishwasher, road sweeper, night clerk.

His first break came as a night operator with the telephone company. In the quiet hours he read books (unlike Christina he read widely and often deeply in several languages), exercised (he never lost his pride in his physical shape; in his sixties he would still invite photographers to take pictures of him stripped to the waist working at his Louis Quinze desk), and listened in on conversations that sounded interesting. Realizing that he was picking up good market tips, he began making notes and studying the financial pages of the newspapers. In a matter of weeks he had made a thousand dollars on one deal and almost half that on another. He invested his winnings in new clothes – and a subscription to a smart rowing club. 'It was,' says his biographer Peter Evans, 'the beginning of a remarkable double life unimagined by his colleagues at the phone company and his drinking pals in La Boca. His new friends at L'Aviron (The Oar) accepted him as a young man with money, good business connections – and loads of charm.'

With a keen eye for the social advancement which would always be important to him, he used that charm to seduce Claudia Muzio. At thirty-five, the Italian soprano was a little past her best, but still a feather in his cap. ('My father was never happy in love, but he was always successful,' Christina once told a friend, adding plaintively: 'With me it is always the other way around.') Only a few months later, when Onassis got into the tobacco business – importing from his father's Athens company a mild Turkish leaf he believed would appeal to women who were taking up smoking – he would shamelessly use her to promote his own brand of cigarettes by smoking them in public. 'She liked my survival strength, but she thought I was a crook,' he would later cheerfully admit to Evans, who recognized that 'his business, his success, his fame, all had their sources in a substratum of sex.'

If Christina would have failed to recognize the Buenos Aires her father knew and loved (he once compared it to 'a charm bracelet made with pieces of the past') and returned to again and again (he kept a permanent suite at the Plaza), she certainly would have been familiar with many of the names. There was Alberto Dodero, for example, the grandfather of the husband of her great friend, Marina. ('Circles inside circles,' Onassis used to tell his daughter. 'Nothing changes inside the best circles.')

Alberto Dodero was a legend in Argentina, and a hero to young Aristotle Onassis. (It was Dodero who first called him Ari, the name which stuck and by which he himself was to become legendary; it was also Dodero, Ari would later tell Christina, 'who destroyed my capacity to be shocked by wealth'.) The youngest of five sons of an Italian immigrant, at the end of World War I, with a tantalizing credit of ten million dollars, Don Alberto had acquired a surplus fleet of United

States ships, resold them immediately at a huge profit and bought a substantial interest in the Mihanovich shipping company. He invited Ari to all his parties and to weekends at his home near Montevideo, across the Rio de la Plata, where sometimes dozens of houseguests would sip Dom Perignon champagne and brunch on *pâté de foie gras* with Perigord truffles flown in fresh from France.

Ari made notes in his little book, he forgot nothing. And Don Alberto's was the style in which one day he himself intended to live.

Dodero introduced Ari to Costa Gratsos, a member of the Dracoulis shipping family. It was Gratsos who began to arouse Ari's interest in shipping. Although tobacco continued to be the major source of his wealth, in 1933, inspired by Dodero's success with the Mihanovich company, and guided by Gratsos's know-how, Ari bought six freighters from the Canadian National Steamship Company. (His first act as a shipowner was to rename two of the vessels *Onassis Penelope* and *Onassis Socrates*, after his parents – his father had died of a heart attack in Athens the year before.)

Shortly after this major shift forward in his fortunes, Ari met and fell deeply in love with Ingeborg Dedichen, the youngest daughter of one of the most respected shipowners in Norway. That he was drawn to beautifully and usefully connected women was obvious; that he was also the kind of man beautiful women go for is confirmed by Ingeborg: 'He liked to lick me between the toes, carefully, like a cat ... he would embrace every part of my body and cover me with kisses before devoting himself to the feet he adored,' she wrote in her autobiography *Onassis, Mon Amour*.

But his active love life did not mean he was neglecting business. Like all Greek shipowners in the 1930s he was a 'dry' carrier, handling cargoes of grain and timber. But the world was changing fast: oil was replacing coal as the number one energy fuel, refineries were multiplying throughout the Middle East. Ari realized that not only were more and more tankers going to be needed to shift the oil to the marketplaces around the world, but also calculated that bigger tankers would mean bigger payloads and lower operating costs. With the help of Ingeborg's influential shipping friends in Norway (who persuaded the Goteborg shipyard to waive 'the Greek clause': minimum 50 per cent cash, maximum five-year credit), Ari commissioned the largest tanker ever built: the 15,000-ton *Ariston*.

The day the *Ariston* was launched in the summer of 1938, Ari revealed that he had ordered an even larger tanker – a 17,500-ton vessel to be called *Buenos Aires*.

The war, when it came in 1939, did not unduly trouble him. He had an Argentine passport, as well as his Greek one, and war can be generous to a neutral shipowner. The Allies were crying out for merchant ships; combat zone rates were sky high, and war-risk policies handsomely covered the losses. It was the closest thing to a one-way bet Ari ever found. In June 1940, leaving his cousin Nicos Konialidis in Buenos Aires to run the tobacco side of things, he headed for New York, the hub of the Allies' maritime world. But when he tried to get into the Union of Greek Shipowners, an imperious and arcane cabal dominated by the first families of Greek shipping, he was blackballed by Stavros Livanos and others who looked down on him as 'a Smyrna upstart', a man who was 'not quite a Greek'.

Also kept out in the cold was a dapper, good-looking young Athenian with hard, gem-like eyes, whose name was Stavros Niarchos.

Their rejection by the old Greeks briefly created a bond between the two men. ('I saw that my enemies were the same as his,' said Ari, who had profoundly felt the injury to his pride and to his sense of self-esteem. 'We had scores to settle with the same bastards.') But their hunger to become accepted, their macho need to flaunt success, their unhideable jealousy of each other, would grow into a fatal and lasting war.

It was a war that Christina would one day join and fight with a vengeance that even Aristotle Onassis himself would stand and watch in awe.

—3—

*Children begin by loving their
parents; after a time they judge
them; rarely, if ever, do they
forgive them*

Oscar Wilde
A Woman of No Importance

SOMETIME IN THE SUMMER OF 1945, when he was forty-five years old, Ari told Costa Gratsos that the die was cast, and that he intended finally to tie the knot. Gratsos naturally imagined that he was going to marry Ingeborg Dedichen, who had followed him to America to set up Mamita Cottage, their home on the north shore of Long Island. But their passionate, often violent affair had now lasted a dozen years and Ingeborg had outlived her usefulness to Ari. And the loyal Gratsos was about to confirm the truth of what he had long suspected, that Ari was ruthless when anything – 'a tanker, a mistress, *anything*' – had served its purpose.

The girl he intended to marry was Athina Livanos.

Fearing that Ari was heading for trouble – Athina was not only barely sixteen years old but also the youngest, the prettiest, and the most beloved daughter of Stavros Livanos, the man whose enmity and influence had kept Ari out of the Union – Gratsos pleaded with him to think again.

But Ari was not merely striving for revenge, nor was he eager for acceptance among the first families of Greek shipping (although both revenge and at least a grudging acceptance would be windfalls of such a union). Athina, or Tina as her friends and family called her, was the prize he wanted most.

Fair-haired with an aquiline nose, finely chiselled mouth, and delicately pencilled eyebrows – the kind of beauty that has all the conviction of good breeding – Tina did not look at all Greek, and in almost every way she was not. Born in London in 1929, she had become a United

19

States citizen during the war, when the Greek shipping establishment fled from London to New York. 'I learned to speak in England, think in New York, and dress in Paris,' she would later tell Lady Carolyn Townshend.

Tina already had a Livanos-blessed interest in John Vatis, a young man close to her own age and a member of an extremely suitable shipping family, and had also caught the eye of Stavros Niarchos, when Ari started to hang around her parents' house at Oyster Bay. And although she was initially amused by his attempts to get her attention with a display of bravado remarkable in a man past forty – diving, water-skiing, balancing one-footed on the saddle of his bicycle – Tina soon became fascinated, and impressed.

Ari took his time. Niarchos, he knew, had rushed his fences (not yet divorced from his second wife Melpomene, he had rashly confessed his interest in Tina to her father) and failed miserably. The crusty, arch-conservative Livanos offered no hope to Ari either. But Ari was not put off by paternal resistance. 'A little opposition is a great help to a fellow sometimes,' he would one day tell Christina, recalling his courting days with her mother. 'No man ever worked his passage in a dead calm,' he said.

He made a point of being nice to both Tina and her older sister, Eugenie, and took care to pay court to their mother, Arietta, a handsome, strong-willed woman of his own age. But it was Tina he took for walks across the Long Island shore. It was Tina who listened to his stories about the past, and about his schemes for the future. And it was Tina to whom he finally proposed – by trailing a streamer behind his speedboat with the letters TILY (Tina I Love You).

'Vulgar, vulgar, vulgar,' sighed Eugenie, the most regally poised member of the family.

Stavros Livanos was furious, not at the proposal itself – despite his dislike of Ari as a man, he had finally rationalized that a Livanos–Onassis shipping alliance was not without its compensations – but because Ari had asked for the wrong daughter. Greek girls wed in order of seniority, he explained when Ari asked for Tina's hand. He added with characteristic directness that he would not object if Ari were to ask for Eugenie's hand instead. 'Your daughters aren't ships, Mr Livanos, you don't dispose of the first of the line first,' Ari is said to have retorted.

Nevertheless, Livanos was sure that Ari would climb down and accept Eugenie. But Ari was adamant and one year later it was the old man who admitted defeat, claiming that he could no longer bear to see Tina looking so sad; he was also probably somewhat encouraged to change his mind by the newly-divorced Niarchos's sudden interest in Eugenie.

On 28 December 1946, Ari and Tina were wed in the Greek cathedral in New York. Tina was seventeen years old, Ari was twenty-three days short of his forty-seventh birthday.

For their honeymoon they took a slow boat to Buenos Aires. The Austrian arms merchant Fritz Mandl gave them a glitzy party at the Plaza. Alberto Dodero invited them to meet Evita Perón. Hollywood film chief Spyros Skouras entertained them at a dinner for one hundred and fifty people. Like all true socialites, Tina knew that to be fêted by the rich and famous was the finest affirmation of her own wealth and celebrity. Among the people she liked best, the society that was the source of her happiness and of Ari's furtherance, Tina had never been so sure of the future.

In March they returned to 16 Sutton Square, a cul-de-sac off Sutton Place in New York City. Tina set about decorating their new home (period French furniture, black marble floors, a Renoir); Ari set about business. Still a 'lone wolf' (his own description of himself), he did much of his work at Sutton Square, making deals and cultivating those who could be useful to him at the parties he and Tina liked to throw. Still only eighteen years old, Tina swiftly established herself as the youngest, the most vivacious and indefatigable hostess in New York.

The 'Golden Greek', the headline writers were beginning to call him, and later on the 'Greek Tycoon'. His rags-to-riches story fascinated the public. They read about *his* parties and *his* deals, about *his* beautiful wife, and *his* magnificent new villa in Montevideo. There was *his* splendid apartment on Avenue Foch in Paris, and *his* villa by the sea outside Athens, and Château de la Croe, a king-size mansion (the Duke and Duchess of Windsor had once lived there) *he* had taken in the South of France. ('My father was the star in our family,' Christina would later tell lover Warren Beatty. 'Everyone else was a contract player.')

Unreported was his heavy drinking. Untalked about was the hatred that had sprung up between him and Stavros Niarchos, who became his brother-in-law at the end of 1947, when he took Eugenie ('the first of the line,' Ari would cruelly call her) for his third wife. It was not simply that when Ari built a tanker, Niarchos built a bigger one. Niarchos also troubled him in ways that transcended business competitiveness. 'Niarchos exuded the *ennui* of the very rich, Onassis had a pauper's *joie de vivre*,' an oil man put his finger on one significant difference between them. Yet the mutual animosity went much deeper than a conflict of styles.

'Both men expected their wives to be loyal in every way, sharing prejudices and enemies, grudges and desires,' wrote Peter Evans in his biography, *Ari*. 'Each man judged the allegiance of their friends by their abhorrence of the other. Ari even forbade Tina to attend Eugenie's wedding to Niarchos. The alienation caused the sisters a lot of pain; Ari saw nothing wrong in his demands.' An Onassis aide added that Ari 'considered forgiveness a weakness and détente a defeat. He needed adversaries. He would have been lost without an enemy to hate ... sometimes the enemy had to be drawn from the closest circle of his own family.'

On 30 April 1948, at the Harkness Pavilion, a private nursing home in New York City, Tina bore her husband a male heir, Alexander, named after Ari's murdered, favourite uncle. Two years off his fiftieth birthday, Ari was duly proud, delighted – 'and perfectly satisfied. We don't plan any more children,' Tina announced with a single-mindedness that caused some friends to feel at least a tremor of apprehension about the state of the marriage; although she added the interesting explanation that Ari believed that 'to have more than one child simply clouds the issue.'

Fifteen months later Tina again became pregnant. Neither she nor Ari wanted the child, but this time Tina was curiously reluctant to agree to an abortion. According to a family source, after at least two such operations since the birth of Alexander, this time she had been warned by her doctor that any more would put at risk her chances of becoming a mother again; still only twenty-one years old, motherhood was clearly an option she might wish to consider with some future husband or lover.

At first, Ari was sure he could talk her into another termination, but the months passed and she continued miserably and mysteriously to carry the unwanted child inside her. Why would she not get rid of it? Ari demanded to know again and again. Unable to admit her reasons to her husband, he became irascible and suspicious and finally violent.

He beat her up not simply in frustration, Tina would tell her future lover Reinaldo Herrera, but in the hope that she would have a miscarriage. 'She said that there was so much blood spilled on the carpet that the stain could never be washed away,' Herrera told the story many years afterwards. 'The carpet finally had to be replaced.'

Christina entered the world – against all the odds, wanted by neither her mother nor her father, 'actually a kind of reproach,' according to Ari's sister Artemis, who knew the truth and loved her most of all – in a New York hospital on 11 December 1950. Her face was Ari's exactly: a likeness that disappointed Tina terribly, but put her husband's mind at rest, at least on one score.

The marriage, in the sense that Tina and Ari had always been together, travelled together, lived under the same roof and shared the same friends, was over. Just as Ari had used Tina's unwelcome pregnancy as a justification for seeing other women, including a shabby one-night affair with Evita Perón arranged by Alberto Dodero for $10,000, so Tina used Ari's infidelity to go her own way. 'He's got his friends and now I'm starting to find mine,' she told Costa Gratsos, who had tried to talk her out of embarking on an affair 'with a totally unsuitable fellow'.

The pattern was set for the next ten years.

'We were like two people killed outright in a car crash ... our car was travelling so fast it carried us on, even when it no longer mattered,' Tina said when she knew herself and Ari so well, and felt their guilt so deeply, that she could only seek to justify their behaviour in sentimental metaphors.

Yet it was the truth, if not entirely the truth. For in their own ways they continued to need each other. If she gave him a touch of class, then Ari gave her the kind of confidence that only experience with a powerful man can bring to a woman. Nevertheless, her affairs were numerous. 'The lack of happiness in my life is hidden by a great deal of pleasure,' she told a French actor whom she had taken up with some ardour while her husband was buying up Monte Carlo and fighting with Prince Rainier.

The 'great deal of pleasure' which disguised Tina's unhappiness clearly did not include the pleasure of motherhood. Neither she nor Ari ever really took to their parental roles. To leave their children, often for months, did not seem to them unkind.

'Christina and Alexander were never a part of their lives, they were always kept in a closet some place,' remembers Wendy Reves, widow of Emery Reves, the millionaire publisher who had first introduced Ari to Sir Winston Churchill at La Pausa, his villa in the South of France. 'I always had the feeling that Tina was in a sense ashamed of having produced such a daughter. I don't think it was given to her to love Christina at all. She almost had a hatred for that child.'

Christina, Wendy Reves added, 'took after her father. She looked like a little Arab child, with huge dark circles under her eyes ... She was very clumsy.' ('For goodness sake, Christina, can't you put your feet together?' she remembered Tina reprimanding the three-year-old child.) 'It was quite different with Alexander. He resembled his mother and was a most attractive boy.' (People who remember the Onassis children at that time tend to make similar points. Churchill's secretary Doreen Pugh recalls that Alexander was 'a charming boy' ... Christina was 'not all that ugly'.)

Christina herself had troubled recollections of her childhood. Looked after by nannies and private tutors, taking her meals with servants, travelling with bodyguards, she had few friends of her own age. She became an uncommunicative child whose awkwardness and natural shyness were often misunderstood as rudeness and put people off. When she was five years old, she suddenly stopped speaking to anyone at all. Tina consulted child psychologists in Zurich, who diagnosed mercurial mutism – and attention-seeking silence often associated with insecure and overprotected children. Years later, confronting this episode, Christina said: 'I guess I didn't talk because I didn't have anything to say.' ('If she had just said "hello" we could have saved $20,000,' Tina complained when she heard the explanation.)

'I keep reading that my dolls were dressed by Dior in the latest fashions from Paris,' Christina would later tell her first husband, Joseph Bolker. 'And they were very nice, but expensive dolls can't replace absent parents when you're four years old.'

But by Christina's sixth birthday, her parents' pragmatic concept of marriage was no longer proving to be the answer for Ari. Before he seemed not to mind Tina's separate life, her dates with handsome young skiers and polo-players and the kind of men who seek the company of rich married ladies. She was the quintessential socialite: 'That's what she does best,' he would growl when the question came up. 'Anyway, she's lousy at housekeeping,' he would often add, to soften the way it sounded. But now in his mid-fifties, drinking harder than ever, richer than he had ever been in his life, he had become beset by all the anxieties of male menopause. Suddenly he could not bear the idea of losing her.

And there was cause for his alarm.

That year Tina had met Reinaldo Herrera at a Rothschild ball in Paris. Although he was some eight years younger, she immediately fell for the Venezuelan's romantic good looks, relaxed sense of fun, his quiet, friendly charm. 'He gives me confidence in my own decisions, and he mades me feel damn good about myself,' she told Eugenie, who was having her own problems with her husband, Niarchos, and understood very well her sister's needs and hopes for the new affair.

Nevertheless, Tina was surprised when Herrera asked to marry her. And more surprised when she heard herself saying yes.

'Ari's not going to want to lose you,' Herrera prophetically warned her. 'You're the best possession he has.'

Ari would have known about the affair from the start. He had Tina watched all the time. And certainly neither of the lovers tried to keep it a secret once the romance had begun. 'Tina and I used to meet in St Moritz, Paris, New York, even on their yacht [the *Christina*] when Ari knew all about us. We talked about the divorce together. He didn't want a divorce, of course. At that time he had some business problems. He felt that everything was going wrong in his life.'

Moreover, this was the first time that Tina had asked him for a divorce in order to marry a lover. At a time, according to Herrera, when Ari was 'not able to function on a sexual level,' the request was a body-blow to his self-esteem.

'We used to talk about the situation until four, five, six o'clock in the morning,' remembers Herrera. 'Rather than a divorce, Ari would propose the most incredible things ... that she should go and live quietly in the country [where both would continue to enjoy her favours]. He had incredible persuasive charm, he was a beguiling man. But the whole thing just became impossible.'

Shortly after this extraordinary episode, in which Ari was proposing shamelessly to share his wife rather than lose her to a younger man, the lovers, confused and perhaps a little unnerved by Ari's response, decided not to see each other for a year. (Still only twenty-one, Herrera was also under pressure from his parents, who were totally opposed to him marrying 'an older woman'.)

But nothing was ever quite what it seemed with Ari. And while he was fighting and scheming for dear life to hold on to Tina (or anyway to keep a face-saving if not a carnal share in her), he was also planning the seduction of Maria Callas, whom he had met for the first time in 1957. 'We are the two most famous living Greeks in the world,' he had told her then, and the idea appealed to him immensely.

Two years later at Contessa Castelbarco's Venice ball, having apparently recovered his ability to function on a sexual level, Ari moved in on Maria with all his charm. The affair ignited almost at once, and became public knowledge in December when he threw a gala party at the Dorchester Hotel for her opening night in *Medea* at Covent Garden.

Maria was cuckolding her husband Giovanni Meneghini but nobody was fooling Tina. She knew exactly what was going on, and how much she was prepared to take. ('I knew the score even before the game began,' she would later explain to Christina.)

But it is unlikely that this and so many other dramas conducted continuously and often quite openly in the saloons and staterooms of the *Christina*, in the drawing-rooms and boudoirs of Avenue Foch and the Château de la Croe – it is unlikely that any of this could have totally escaped the attention of little Christina, even if she did not yet understand the finer points of *les liaisons dangereuses*.

'She was a sensitive child, a thoughtful, introspective little thing,' said one frequent English guest on the Onassis yacht and at the château throughout this tumultuous time. 'And the aura of stress between Ari and Tina, even when they were putting on a show of togetherness for Churchill, or the Rainiers, or whoever the hell it was they wanted to impress, was quite palpable. Sometimes you would suddenly notice her sitting there, Christina, on the sidelines, under the trees, watching, not saying a word, taking it all in. Very little escaped her, believe me. Sometimes you'd see a glance between her and Alexander. People said they didn't get on, and that they didn't understand each other. I think they understood each other and what was going on perfectly. After all, they were casualties together.'

But family casualties were so small a part of the big drama Ari and Tina were playing out between themselves that they did not notice them at all.

'The hypocrisies and deceits of our parents are sometimes harder to bear than watching them have a knock-down drag-out brawl,' Christina later told a girlfriend in Paris, who was going through a messy divorce and worrying about the effect it might have on her two small children.

In November 1959, ten days after Meneghini got a legal separation from Callas in Italy (his writ of application did not name Ari, referring only to Callas's abrupt transformation from a 'loyal and grateful wife' to one whose behaviour was 'incompatible with elementary decency' following a cruise with 'persons who are reckoned the most powerful of our time'), Tina filed for divorce in the New York State Supreme Court on the grounds of adultery, claiming custody of Christina and Alexander. In a brief, valedictory statement issued through her New York lawyers, Tina said:

'It is almost thirteen years since Mr Onassis and I were married in New York City. Since then he has become one of the world's richest men, but his great wealth has not brought me happiness with him nor, as the world knows, has it brought him happiness with me. After we parted this summer in Venice, I had hoped that Mr Onassis loved our children enough and respected our privacy sufficiently to meet with me – or, through lawyers, with my lawyers – to straighten out our problems. But that was not to be.

'Mr Onassis knows positively that I want none of his wealth and that I am solely concerned with the welfare of our children.'

Deeply regretting that 'Mr Onassis' had left her no alternative other than a suit for divorce, and wishing him well, Tina asked to be left with her children in peace.

—4—

Society is a hospital of incurables

Ralph Waldo Emerson
New England Reformers

THE OLD GREEKS REVERED THE APPEARANCE of respectability almost as much as they respected the reality of money. And to mollify her father, who feared that 'a smutty divorce' would both harm her and the children and upset his friends, Tina agreed to drop the New York action with its necessary allegation of adultery (she had cited not Callas but old schoolfriend Jeanne Rhinelander, with whom she had caught Ari one afternoon in bed at the Château de la Croe). In June 1960, in Alabama, she was granted an uncontested quickie divorce on the grounds of mental cruelty.

To celebrate her independence, she gave a dinner party at the Hôtel de Paris in Monte Carlo to announce that in future she would be known as Tina Livanos. 'I'm sound in wind and limb and fancy free,' she told her sister, Eugenie Niarchos, who was beginning to express a yearning for a similar freedom. 'I'm quite the happiest I've been in thirteen years,' Tina insisted in her stunning English accent.

Happiness for Tina was the social merry-go-round, and it had never spun so fast as it did in the next six months. She celebrated the New Year skiing with Christina and Alexander in St Moritz. When the children returned to their schools in Paris, Tina took off for some end-of-season pheasant shooting on the Earl of Durham's estate in England. In February she flew back to Switzerland. It was her favourite month in St Moritz. Apart from the excitement of the Bob and Cresta Runs, and polo on the iced lake, in February St Moritz was the *only* place to be seen. The Shah of Iran, Gianni Agnelli, Baron Heini Thyssen would all be in town.

But February can also be the cruellest month, even for the rich. Skiing down the Niarchos Couloir run from the 3,057-metre-high Priz-Nair station, she fell and catapulted thirty feet, shattering her right leg. At the Klinik Bernhard, the fractures were considered to be so serious that Stavros Niarchos, whose first pick of the Livanos sisters she had once been, immediately sent his Grumman-Gulfstream to England to fetch the brilliant bone specialist Professor Joseph Trueta to take charge of the case.

After a three-hour examination, Trueta, the head of the Nuffield Orthopaedic Centre in Oxford, identified eighteen separate fractures; in addition to which, Tina had a badly fractured knee. After the operation, Tina remained at the Klinik until 7 March, when it was considered safe for her to be flown to Oxford, where she was to continue her recuperation under the personal supervision of Trueta.

Her leg would be in plaster for three months, but because of the severity of the damage to her knee, she was told that she might have to walk with a cane for a year. 'Now I'm only sound in wind and fancy free!' she cabled her sister from Oxford, where she had been flown in her ever-attentive brother-in-law's private plane.

After the first drama and excitement of the accident, the press attention, Ari's visit to Oxford, which had encouraged fresh rumours that they were to remarry (infuriating Maria Callas, Tina heard with satisfaction), Tina became immensely bored, and quite depressed when she faced up to the reality of a long stay in the Nuffield.

Oxford was very nice but it was not St Moritz, nor was it Paris or New York or the South of France, and visitors, her kind of visitors, were hard to come by. Christina, now eleven years old, was brought over for a day from Switzerland but that was not the same thing at all.

There is nothing quite so lonely as a lonely socialite. Tina's brother George, who knew this, had recently gone to work in the family's London office, and remembered his friend Sunny Blandford, who lived conveniently close to Oxford, at Lee Place in Charlbury, on the edge of the Blenheim Palace estate. Would he drop by for an hour or two to cheer his sister up? George enquired. Sunny, a 6 ft 2 ins former Life Guards officer, a.k.a. the Marquess of Blandford (he got the sobriquet 'Sunny' when he held the courtesy title of the Earl of Sunderland), agreed at once.

It is unlikely that Tina would have had to reach for her *Debrett's* to have at least a passing knowledge of the Marquess. Belonging to one of the finest families in the land, he was the son of the 10th Duke of Marlborough, whose ancestor had been John Churchill, Queen Anne's celebrated general, victor of the battles of Blenheim, Ramillies, Oudenarde and Malplaquet, for which a grateful nation gave him the Royal Manor of Woodstock and commissioned Vanbrugh to build the magnificent palace. Sir Winston Churchill, at that very moment yachting with Ari in the Caribbean, was the grandson of the 7th duke, and had been born at Blenheim. One day Sunny would be the 11th duke.

That all this history excited her romantic imagination is in no doubt. Shortly after Sunny's first visit to her bedside, carrying an enormous bunch of flowers, Tina called her former young lover Reinaldo Herrera in New York and told him that she had just met 'the nicest man', and planned to marry him.

'Are you in love with him?' asked Herrera, who had long ago accepted the fact that their trial separation had become a permanent thing.

'No,' she answered truthfully. 'But I am very fond of him, you see.'

Added to all Sunny's other wonderful advantages in life, Tina was bound to have noticed, was a marriage that had recently been dissolved. Timing, Ari used to say, was everything in life; and on reflection Tina was beginning to think less badly about her broken leg. (Perhaps the only small worry in her mind, for she was still a superstitious Greek at heart, was the thought that the leg had been in plaster the very first time she met Ari in New York.)

In the following weeks, Sunny became a regular visitor to Tina's bedside and several times a week took her for car rides through the narrow Oxfordshire lanes. When she finally returned to Paris on 12 April, the friendship had sufficiently progressed for her to tell Christina and Alexander about the new friend in her life, although she insisted, perhaps out of respect for their father, perhaps to get them gradually used to the idea of Sunny, that there was no question of a serious romance.

Certainly the future 11th duke kept out of the way in England while Tina, ensconced in her large new apartment on Avenue Gabriel, next to the Elysée Palace, spent time with her children, and got accustomed to her crutches. But neither children nor crutches held a limitless fascination for Tina, and Stavros Niarchos's invitation to take a recuperative voyage in the Mediterranean aboard his black-hulled schooner

Creole 'came none too soon,' she said.

Happy to be getting back into the swim of things, she was looking relaxed and sure of herself and delicately tanned (she had an English lady's repressed horror of looking 'too Mediterranean') when she returned to Oxford in June for Professor Trueta to remove the plaster. Sunny was there to hold her hand.

That evening Tina cabled her sister in Paris, 'Sound in wind and limb again – but don't imagine remaining fancy free for long!'

During the next weeks, Sunny became her inseparable companion. She met his two children – James, the Earl of Sunderland, who was then six years old, and Lady Henrietta Spencer Churchill, aged three – of whom Sunny had custody.

In September, on Niarchos's Aegean island, Spetsopoula, the marriage was arranged and thoroughly approved of by the 10th Duke of Marl-borough (Bert, to his friends), who believed that multi-millionairesses were blessings conferred upon the aristocracy, if not by God then by Croesus.

Tina and the Marquess were married in a Greek Orthodox ceremony in Paris on 23 October. Over one hundred photographers and reporters covered the service, turning it into what the bride later called 'a dreadful, rowdy shambles'. Christina was photographed wearing a fur hat bought for her in Moscow by her father and which she wore, she would claim later, 'as a secret sign of allegiance to him'. Not that she had anything against Sunny; she took to him from the first, but there is always something a little past bearing when you are eleven years old and your mother marries again.

Seventeenth-century Lee Place, which was to be Christina's home for the next seven years, was an impressive house but no more so than the Château de la Croe in the South of France, whose ceilings were higher and as finely carved, and whose bedrooms were larger, more numerous, and warmer, too. There were fewer servants than she had been used to at the chateau and aboard the *Christina* (the marquess, even after his new father-in-law, Stavros Livanos, had given him a job in the family business, made do with one chauffeur, a solitary chef, a butler, and a single nanny shared between James and Henrietta); but Christina, accompanied by Miss Lehane, a governess so redoubtable and strict that nobody ever knew her first name, did not complain.

Christina had lost a great deal of her early shyness and quickly became fond of and relaxed with her stepbrother and stepsister. Her pet name for her illustrious stepfather was Sunbun, whom she adored to tease and continued to tease all her life. 'When she went to London, when she was older, she often went on the train from Charlbury,' recalls James. 'She loved the novelty of that. At dinner she would say to Daddy, "Do you know what, Sunbun, I went third class." Or, "Do you know what, Sunbun, I didn't pay the fare and almost got arrested by the guard. But it was all right – I dropped your name." She used to like to get a reaction, to shock people,' he said.

'I didn't realize how alone I had been until I moved to Lee Place,' Christina said later. 'James and Henrietta, although there were three years between them, had a family sense of sharing and belonging between them. It brought home to me the fact that I never had that. I had a brother and I had a mother and father who were usually somewhere else, and usually apart. We lived like people who occasionally stayed in the same expensive hotel, and occasionally bumped into each other.' ('She loved Lee Place and when we had dinner latterly in London she would reflect about those days,' said James. 'She was in a trance one evening – we were having dinner at Pier 31 – and I said, "What are you thinking about?" She said, "Those days."')

Life at Lee Place settled into a routine that was a perfect synthesis of Greek largesse and aristocratic goodwill. Having improved the décor with a few Renoirs, a brace of Pissarros, and a rather splendid Monet, Tina set about recapturing some of her New York reputation as a hostess. Her weekend parties became renowned. After dinner, guests watched the latest movies in the private screening room she had built on to the house. 'We knew Tina was rich,' remembers stepson James, now himself the Marquess of Blandford (he inherited his father's second title when Sunny became the 11th duke). 'There was no shortage of anything.'

Shooting parties from October to January were interrupted only for the Christmas holidays, spent in St Moritz at the splendidly named Villa Relaxez-Vous, which had been put at Tina's permanent disposal by Stavros Niarchos, and where Christina looked forward to catching up with her Niarchos cousins, Philippe, Spyros, Constantine and Maria. February, of course, meant St Moritz again, followed by Paris in the spring. The months of July and September were spent on Spetsopoula. 'One day you will learn that there is something splendidly reassuring about routine,' Tina told her daughter, who had complained that her year was as predictable as her daily journey to and from Headington Girls' School in nearby Oxford.

Tina's quiet hopes of turning her daughter into something akin to an English lady (by osmosis, if all else failed) never let up. On summer weekends, together with her stepsister Lady Henrietta, Christina competed in all the local gymkhanas, and spent hours grooming her pony, a grey named Cobby. She played tennis with enthusiasm, but no perceptible talent; she swam every day in the heated pool. And although she was already beginning to be teased because of her gargantuan appetite ('she was always gorging herself,' remembers James Blandford), and her unusual consumption of Coca-Cola, there was no sign of the weight problems that would trouble her in the years to come.

'Christina was never a beauty, but she could look quite good at that time,' says James, recalling the moment he realized that she was growing into a young woman. Shortly after her fifteenth birthday she returned from her boarding school in Switzerland (she had left Headington for St George's two years before) with a great 'pash' – St George's school slang for passion – for a young Greek she had met with her father in Paris.

His name was Peter Goulandris. The Goulandris family owned four shipping lines, totalling over 135 vessels with a value in excess of $1.5 billion; Christina recited the vital statistics, learned from her father, who thoroughly approved of young Goulandris. His mother, Maria, a dominant personality who had raised Peter and his sister, Chrysanthe, after their father died when they were children, was a member of the distinguished, and even richer, Lemos family. And Maria, unfortunately, did not approve of Onassis at all. However, her son was openly sweet on Christina and the friendship was allowed to continue during Christina's vacations.

Now that she was becoming a young woman, Christina was seeing a great deal more of her father. 'It is sad that now I need him less, he wants to see me more,' she told Alexander when they met aboard the *Christina* in the summer of 1964, shortly after she had accompanied Ari to the wedding in Paris of Florence Michard-Pelissier, the eldest daughter of his lawyer, to the French tennis champion Jean-Noël Grinda. Jean-Noël's sister, Francine, was married to pharmaceutical heir Henri Roussel, who was accompanied by his daughter, Christine – and his eleven-year-old son, Thierry. Later Christina liked to tell how, when her brother had enquired whether she had met anybody interesting at the wedding, she had said: 'The place was full of schoolkids!'

Their separate lives were marked in the diverse personalities of Christina and Alexander. At that time, her ordered and conservative family-oriented existence at Lee Place still influenced her behaviour and most people who met her in the 1960s remember her politeness, her quiet-spokenness – and the fact that 'she didn't come on like a rich kid at all.' (At this time she was still careful with her allowance of $4,000 a month; the most extravagant thing she had ever done was to have a Coke machine installed at St George's.)

Alexander, according to one Paris friend, was the worst kind of rich kid: 'He was cocky with it. He was really quite a shit.'

But he was more complex and more interesting than that.

Despite being set up with his own tutor and a private apartment in a Paris hotel at sixteen, he failed his exams at the *lycée* after returning late from a dirty weekend in St Tropez. Although Ari took pride in his son's sexual escapades, he was furious at his failure. Refusing to 'waste money educating a lazy kid,' he put him to work in his Monaco office, on a shoestring salary of $12,000 a year plus expenses. Later Alexander said that there had never been a day when he had 'not been intimidated' by Ari's wealth. And although in Monte Carlo he began to appreciate the miracle his father had performed in creating that extraordinary empire, his disaffection was slowly turning to hostility and hatred. Driving fast through the night he later said was his way of expiating the anger and inadequacy with which he was tormented.

In the summer of 1966, with Christina and their friend Taki Theodoracopulos, he set off in his Ferrari (a gift from his unpredictable father for passing his driving test) for a lunch date in Antibes. They had barely got out of Monte Carlo when it became clear to both Christina and Taki that Alexander was intent upon impressing them with his racing skills. Christina began to scream and plead with him to slow down. Taki, at that time in his mid-twenties and a tennis-player who had represented Greece, was determined not to show his own fear and sat grim-faced as Alexander pushed the car to its limit on the twisting corniche road.

The accident was not long coming. Unable to hold a bend in the narrow road, Alexander sideswiped an oncoming car.

The other driver, an elderly Russian Jew, obviously badly shaken, looked ashen when he saw the damage done to Alexander's expensive car. He began nervously apologizing and taking the blame for the whole thing. Alexander recognized an opportunity when he saw one. 'What's your name, buddy?' he asked in a tone that Taki immediately recognized as a perfect imitation of his father.

'Serge Lifar,' said the old man.

The name of the legendary former ballet dancer and choreographer meant nothing to Alexander, nor to Christina, who was taking her brother's side in the matter. Taki tried to intercede. But having learned that the old man, whose car was old and almost valueless, had no insurance and no driving licence, Alexander was in full cry, determined to sue for damages to his Ferrari.

When the case came to court, Alexander called Taki as a witness. But Theodoracopulos, like most amateur sportsmen, believed in fair play. His testimony was wholly on the side of Serge Lifar.

Alexander lost the case. Alexander never spoke to Taki again.

'Neither of the Onassis children have the slightest idea what moral behaviour is all about,' Taki told his father afterwards. 'They may have the best nannies and tutors but children acquire morality not from the hired help but from the example of their parents.'

———

The days when Christina would automatically look to her mother for guidance and example were rapidly running out – just as Tina's days as an English marchioness were coming to an end. And the recent closeness Christina had found with her father, whose devotion she had started to trust, was almost over, too.

Almost eighteen years old, she was on the threshold of the years when she would be, as she later put it in a vivid phrase, 'living among so many hurts'.

Tina had grown tired of England. England and English country life and its parochial problems had become deeply unattractive to her. Harold Wilson's Labour government, which had come to power in 1964 promising to 'squeeze the rich until the pips squeak', was even less appealing. The 'reassurance of routine', in which she put so much trust, had finally let her down. She hated the unpredictable English weather; she loathed the shooting, which, it seemed to her, more and more took place in freezing rain and cold; she detested wet gun-dogs shaking themselves all over the furniture. ('Be happy with what you've got – the aristocracy is all wet,' she cabled Eugenie at this time; her sister still enjoyed Tina's schoolgirl humour, and needed cheering up as her own marriage to Stavros Niarchos continued its bumpy ride.)

But Tina had never been deeply in love with Sunny, and it was not the hardest or the saddest decision she ever had to make in her life.

'She got claustrophobic, then she started to go walkabout,' James Blandford, who had been close to his stepmother (she wrote him every week when he went away to school, while Christina said she could count her mother's letters 'on the fingers of one hand'), recalled the beginning of the end of her marriage to his father. 'I remember we were in George [Livanos]'s house in St Moritz and Tina was doing her hair with Carmen rollers. Daddy had gone back to England, they weren't spending a lot of time together. I said to her, "When are you coming back to Lee Place?" And she said, "I'm not."'

Although still not fourteen years old at that time, Blandford saw the situation with a clarity and an understanding that would have been unusual in somebody twice his age. 'Daddy is not a great maker of an effort,' he said. 'If you marry into money and you want that type of life, you toe the line. And if you don't want it, you don't. My father didn't.'

———

Secrecy was at the heart of all Ari's most serious ambitions, and it was not surprising that he had not even hinted to his daughter at his intention to take a new wife. And although Christina knew that Jacqueline Kennedy and her sister Princess Lee Radziwill (with whom she knew her father was having 'a little walk-out on the q.t.') were part of the new crowd surrounding Ari, Maria Callas was still his 'woman' – still blaming her for breaking up her parents' marriage, Christina found it hard even to utter her name. And if he were to marry again, and she prayed that he would not, as sure as anything 'the woman' would be the one. (Alexander referred to her as the Singer, just as later he would dub his stepmother the Widow.)

Her father's recent unusual air of preoccupation, his several unexplained trips to America (a country he did not care for in the ordinary way), may have passed her by, however. For she had a more personal problem on her mind. For several years her mother had been telling her that as soon as her face reached maturity she must have plastic surgery on her nose, which was the nose of a hawk, unattractive from every aspect, inherited from Ari. (Tina's nose, 'a little like Pinocchio's,' she thought, had been acquired after a car accident in Switzerland, and gave her the *gamine* look that had been fashionable in the 1950s.)

The operation was performed in Paris, and judged a great success. The darkness under her eyes had also been removed. Her convalescence was spent on Coronis, her uncle George Livanos's new island close to Spetsopoula, where her mother now had a house which, it was becoming an open secret, she preferred to Lee Place. (*'Liking* somebody,' she was heard to observe, 'simply *isn't* enough to sustain a live-in relationship.')

Her face healed, Christina returned to Paris saying that she felt 'like a million dollars' – a modest appraisal in her case, but wholly satisfactory to her.

But her new face, which had given her so much more confidence and a new dimension of happiness, was suddenly forgotten with the news that her father was to remarry – not his 'woman', but Jacqueline Kennedy, widow of the thirty-fifth president of the United States. An ageing millionaire in the grip of passion is a natural source of worry to his heirs, and Ari had purposely given his children little time to fret or to adjust to the idea of Jackie, telling them of his plans only a matter of days before the wedding.

Christina wept. Alexander left the house and drove his Ferrari at great speed through the night. Nevertheless, they both attended the ceremony on Skorpios on 20 October 1968. 'It's a perfect match,' Alexander reassured his little sister. 'Our father loves names and Jackie loves money.'

—5—

*For this is the sort of engagement, you
see,
That is binding on you but not binding
on me*

William Allen Butler
Nothing to Wear

ARISTOTLE ONASSIS NEVER STOPPED SCHEMING. He had a compulsive need to control and pressure people to his way of thinking, even when those people were those he loved most. And in the autumn of 1969, putting aside the problems that were surfacing in his new marriage, he decided it was time to take an active part in Christina's affairs. 'She needs a father's hand,' he told Costa Gratsos, who was his closest aide, 'now that Tina is too wrapped up in her divorce to care about her.'

Believing that she was doing very well on her own, it was an offer that Christina was determined to refuse. Her friendship with Peter Goulandris had moved from childhood infatuation to a tender teenage romance. Peter's mother, the formidable Maria, continued to disapprove of the relationship (nothing could dissuade her from the view that Ari was a common adventurer whose behaviour had brought opprobrium on the great Greek shipping families), but she did nothing to stop them seeing each other as long as their friendship remained platonic. And platonic it had remained.

Whether he was obeying his mother's wishes or observing some gentlemanly Lemos–Goulandris code, Peter seemed uncommonly reluctant to seduce Christina. And it worried Christina dreadfully. That she was still a virgin at nineteen might please her father, who constantly sought her assurance on the subject, but it did not please Christina, who was now working in the New York office of Olympic Airways, the Greek national airline which her father had started in 1957.

And as usual, her thoughts were only of Peter Goulandris when she flew to St Moritz for the Christmas vacation in 1969. That year it had been arranged for her to stay at the Villa Bambi, with uncle George.

Like many second-generation shipping Greeks, George Livanos was educated in America (St Paul's in Concorde, New Hampshire, then the University of Virginia) and had many American friends and acquaintances, some of whom regularly turned up in St Moritz for the winter sports, and some of whom were almost as rich as George himself. Among them was former St Paul's classmate Tommy Ford, whose mother was the heiress to a Pittsburgh plate glass fortune. His best friend was Danny Marentette, another regular in St Moritz, and also a man of private means.

Sharing similar backgrounds and interests, the three men became regular companions in St Moritz, and met for lunch each day at the Corviglia Club. High above the town and reached by two cable-car journeys, the club was *the* place to be seen; membership was $6,000 a year, and so exclusive that only the richest and most 'social incasts' – Christina's pet name for Corviglia's elegant set – could even hope to get onto the waiting list.

It was here one lunchtime that Christina and Danny Marentette met. Introduced by George, Marentette invited her to join his table. He had just come from a month of big-game hunting in Kenya with Walter Buell Ford, a nephew of Henry Ford II, and his wife Barbara. They had shot elephants, lions and leopards. Perhaps suspecting some suppressed horror in Christina, Marentette explained his theory and justification that shooting was a culling process, and vital to the survival of the animals they were killing. (It was a familiar argument; Christina had heard her father use it many times to justify his whale hunts in the 1950s.)

What impressed her most about Danny Marentette was the way he constantly brought her into the conversation – there were about a dozen people at the table, all men – and treated her both as an equal and as a woman (most of her girlfriends were still in college or school). Certainly she was impressed enough to change her mind about quitting for the day and accept his invitation to ski down from the club.

Christina noticed that Marentette, who was slight and of medium height, walked with a limp (caused by a congenital hip disorder), and she was surprised when he skied so well. He skied like an expert, which indeed he was. Herself a very fine off-piste skier, she had trouble staying with him on the descent from the club. As she climbed into the car waiting for her at the bottom of the run, she invited him to dinner at Villa Bambi the following night. 'We always have a film show after dinner,' she added hastily, perhaps fearful that she was not attraction enough. 'George has the latest movies flown over.' Never wholly confident about her looks, she was especially apprehensive at this time. 'It takes about five years after you've had your nose fixed before you can relax and accept that you no longer look the way you did as a kid,' she would later confide to a girlfriend.

Marentette accepted her invitation, and the next. Soon they were daily companions. 'George flew off in his helicopter to find the best snow, but Christina said, "I don't want the helicopter, it's too big deal. We'll use the lifts just like anybody else,"' Marentette remembered their first day together. 'Willy, George's personal ski instructor, the only Swiss I know with a sense of humour, we're driving along in his Volkswagen, and he's saying: "We're such simple folk. We don't even take the helicopter to ski."'

But Christina's determination to behave and be treated like anybody else became short-lived when she realized that without the seclusion of the Livanos helicopter she was vulnerable to the attentions of the paparazzi photographers. 'When we got out of the car at the foot of the Corvatsch there were photographers everywhere,' said Marentette. 'And it's Sunday, and there's a line which has to be two hours long . . . English, Italians, Germans Swiss, Americans.

'"Never mind," she said. "My uncle Stavros owns this mountain and everything on it."

'We went straight to the front of the line! Forget being like everyone else!'

Their days together were tremendous fun. Discovering that Marentette shared a similar sense of humour to her own was an unexpected bonus. Noticing an overweight German in a restaurant about to tuck into a plate of sausages, she said: 'Willy, I'll give you one hundred dollars if you go over to that table, pick up a bratwurst, and take a big bite out of it.' He did. Christina paid up with pleasure to see Marentette laugh so hard.

They dined every night, either at the Villa Bambi or with friends in restaurants, but always ending up in the King's Club discothèque in the basement of the Palace Hotel, where they would talk and dance until the small hours. Always totally honest with people she liked, Christina told him all about Peter Goulandris, and the problem he appeared to be having in taking her to bed. It was, she continued with the guilelessness that was her foible in such intimate matters, his problem and not hers.

But to friends it appeared that Danny was swiftly supplanting Goulandris in her affections. 'Christina was taking things from him that I didn't expect to see her take from anybody,' said a friend who watched the relationship in St Moritz grow. 'Danny definitely had the whip hand. He didn't let her get away with a thing. He could bring her down to earth with *a look*. She was enjoying every minute.'

Within a week Danny Marentette had become her first lover.

It was the worst possible news for Ari, who knew everything about the affair. Before Christina had even slept with Marentette, he had a file on the young American. He knew that he was moderately well-off (judging his wealth on the Onassian scale), was educated at Choate (the Connecticut prep school favoured by his wife's former Kennedy inlaws); his family lived in Grosse Point, Detroit's best suburb, and his father Lloyd had a plastics company. His mother Margaret had inherited a fortune based on newspapers and six television stations; her greatgrandfather was James Scripps, founder of the *Detroit News;* his halfbrother E. W. Scripps had started the Scripps-Howard papers, now the largest chain in America. Danny had not gone into either of the family businesses. After spells at Virginia and Columbia universities he was living in New York. He was presently working as a bloodstock agent, and also owned a string of racehorses.

A father might discover worse things about a daughter's lover. Even so, it was still not good news for Ari. For he had been having talks with Peter Goulandris and, albeit without the formidable Maria's blessing, it was agreed that Peter's engagement to Christina would be announced in April in a statement to be issued from Skorpios.

Now with so much at risk (the Goulandris shipping lines, 135 vessels, $1.5 billion), Ari ordered Christina to return at once to Skorpios for a heart-to-heart. In the event, he became incapable of rational discussion, and berated his daughter for her inconsiderate passion, accusing her of being 'a little whore', and forbidding her to return to New York or ever to see Danny Marentette again.

'Loving isn't a business deal,' she screamed back at him, pleading to be given the dignity of her own decision. Yet she was not surprised by his violent reaction. Almost as heady as his need to wheel and deal were his dreams of dynastic grandeur. And so, in spite of Christina's protests and tears, and still secure in his ultimate power over his family, Ari confidently leaked rumours of the impending engagement.

The day before the engagement was to be officially announced, Christina flew to New York and Danny Marentette.

Publicly amused and excusing her hasty decampment as something he called 'nervous dyspepsia', Ari was privately incandescent with rage, and on 26 April dispatched Jackie to New York to 'talk some sense into the girl'. Greek newspapers, briefed by his people in Athens, described Jackie's journey as 'an errand of romance', and continued confidently to speculate on the forthcoming alliance between the Onassis and Goulandris families.

But it was not to be. By the time Jackie caught up with her step-daughter in New York, Christina had got confirmation of what she had suspected for several weeks. 'Tell my father I'm pregnant,' she told Jackie. 'Tell him I intend to keep the baby, and that Danny and I are going to be married.' (It must have been the last thing Jackie wanted to hear. Conscious of her husband's willingness to blame the messenger in such matters, she got Costa Gratsos in New York to pass on the tidings of Ari's impending grandfatherhood and contrived to remain in America until the dust had settled on Skorpios.)

Christina loved the Big Apple. Marentette had an apartment on the Upper East Side, but remarkably, given her condition and their stated intent, Christina stayed in the apartment Ari kept at the Pierre Hotel. But the young lovers had a great time. In the early mornings they went out to Belmont to watch Marentette's horses in training. They lunched most days at P. J. Clarke's saloon on Third Avenue, one of her father's favourite watering-holes; the evenings were spent dining and dancing in whatever latest place took her fancy. But Christina was beginning to prove pretty rich even for the blood of a 'moderately well-off' fellow like Marentette. 'Rich girls are much more expensive to go around with than poor girls,' he ruefully reflected not long ago. 'You have to pick up the tab all the time to prove you're not simply after their money!'

As soon as she knew she was pregnant, Christina had called her mother in London to give her the news. Tina invited her and Danny to 'come and talk about it at once'. She wasn't *personally* against the idea, she said, but there were things that had to be discussed, and questions of inheritance that would have to be settled with Ari. 'Your father isn't going to like this,' Tina said, pointing out that there was 'little room for people with names like Marentette' in the familial ecology of Greek shipping. Christina said she knew that, but she loved him all the same.

For a few days in London, all seemed to be going well for Christina and Danny. They picked up the social round where they had left off in New York. Dining and dancing at Annabel's, they appeared not to have a care in the world. They even stayed openly together at Christina's small Mayfair house in Reeves Mews. Tina, with a proper respect for the proprieties, put in a rare appearance at Lee Place in order to invite them down for the weekend. Christina told her mother that they were thinking of flying to Baltimore, where the state marriage laws were reasonably relaxed, and not too many questions were asked about under-aged heiresses. Tina wisely advised against it.

The situation altered dramatically when at the beginning of May, Eugenie Niarchos was found dead in her bedroom on Spetsopoula. She had apparently committed suicide and the shock waves were felt throughout the two families.

Aunt Eugenie had been a big favourite of Christina, who took the news especially badly. But the tragedy in the Aegean was the excuse Tina wanted in order to side openly with Ari. She urged Christina to reconsider her plans. Marriage was a big step and could not be taken lightly. It was so easy to make a mistake when you are young. Poor Eugenie had made a mistake and now she was dead. Aunt Artemis discreetly pleaded with her to 'postpone your plans' out of respect for Eugenie's memory. Ari softened his line too, asking his daughter to 'listen to your mother, just do that for me.' Danny also was having doubts, and feeling the pressure. The lobbying, conducted in a strangely conflicting atmosphere of grief and urgency, became at last irresistible.

At the beginning of June, Christina booked into a Wimpole Street clinic. The operation cost forty pounds. Tina thought that was a very reasonable price to pay for an abortion. 'I paid much more than that in New York twenty years ago,' she told her daughter.

The young lovers met three weeks later at Royal Ascot. Christina looked tremendous in her Ascot finery; Danny, in traditional top hat and tails, must still have been a romantic figure to her. But they both knew it was over between them. 'We never saw each other again,' said Marentette. He has never married.

The death of Eugenie changed all their lives. A family already split by rivalry and divorce was now divided by suspicion and hatred. Ari was sure that Eugenie had been murdered, and lost no time in convincing Christina that he was right. Certainly the circumstances of the death on Spetsopoula were strange, and the explanations confused and unsatisfactory in the days that followed.

After taking twenty-five Seconal tablets, Eugenie wrote Stavros in red pencil, in English: 'For the first time in all our life together I have begged you to help me. I have implored you. The error is mine. But sometimes one must forgive and forget.' Later she switched to a ballpoint pen and added a cryptic, almost indecipherable, postscript: '26 is an unlucky number. It is the double of 12.10b of whisky.'

Niarchos discovered his wife unconscious in her room at 10.25 p.m. on the evening of 3 May. Realizing at once that she had overdosed, as she had done several times before, he began shaking and slapping her in an attempt to bring her round; when she slipped to the floor, he took her by the neck and hauled her upright. She fell several times in the struggle to get her back on the bed. He called for black coffee and with the help of his valet, Angelo Marchini, attempted to pour it down her throat. It was more than half an hour before he telephoned his sister, Maria Dracopoulos, in Athens and urged her to send the company physician. At 12.25 a.m. Dr Panayotis Arnautis pronounced Eugenie dead. She was forty-four years old.

Since death was not from natural causes, Dr Arnautis refused to issue a death certificate, and the body was flown to Athens for a post mortem examination. The autopsy report listed multiple injuries to Eugenie's body, including a two-inch bruise on the abdomen with internal bleeding and bleeding behind the diaphragm in the area of the fourth and fifth vertebrae; a bruise on the left eye and swelling on the left temple; an elliptic haemorrhage on the right side of her neck; a haemorrhage to the left of her larynx with small contusions above the collarbone on the left side of her neck; and there was also bruising to her left arm, ankle and shin.

All these injuries were consistent with strenuous attempts at resuscitation, concluded Dr Georgios Agioutantis, professor of forensic medicine at Athens University, and Dr Demetrios Kapsakis, director of the Department of Forensic Medicine in the Ministry of Justice. Death, they concluded, was caused by an overdose of barbiturates.

But Ari's suspicions would not go away. He continued to spread scurrilous rumours and agitate to keep the case alive. 'Why the hell did Stavros wait so long?' he would rasp. 'Why did he have to send all the way to Athens for a doctor when there was a doctor minutes away on Spetsai? Couldn't he see his wife was *dying?*'

He was triumphant when a second autopsy, ordered by the Piraeus public prosecutor, found that the Seconal in Eugenie's body (two milligrams of barbiturate in one hundred cubic centimetres of blood) was not a lethal dose and that her death resulted from physical injuries. Ari kept up the pressure, and on 21 August the public prosecutor recommended that Niarchos be charged with causing bodily injuries leading to his wife's death. He proposed that the sixty-year-old shipowner be tried under Article 311 of the Greek penal code: involuntary homicide, which carries on conviction a maximum penalty of eighteen years in prison. But when the proposed indictment was submitted to the High Court in Athens for approval, the judges ruled that the evidence merely confirmed that Eugenie Niarchos had taken her own life and the case was closed.

But the Spetsopoula incident was more than a family scandal; potentially it had been a political one as well. Ari was competing tooth and nail with Niarchos for multi-million dollar deals with the Greek military junta. He knew that as long as there was a breath of scandal in the air, the Greek dictator George Papadopoulos, who was Ari's man, and a conspirator by instinct, would be only too willing to delay the ratification of Niarchos's massive refinery deal, since Niarchos's patron was his rival, Colonel Makarezos. Eugenie's death was fair game to Ari.

His motives were obvious to more sophisticated minds than Christina's, and she continued to be deeply depressed and confused by the death on Spetsopoula. Moreover, it was the first time she had seen her father's hatred in action. Although she continued to blame Niarchos for her aunt's death, she did not like what her father was doing.

Throughout the whole drama, Tina had been loyally and, some believed, inexplicably on the side of Stavros; even Ariette stuck by her beleaguered son-in-law. But both women knew that Eugenie – a lovely, fragile woman – had become deeply unstable. In one outburst she had accused Tina of having an affair with her husband; an accusation strenuously denied by both Tina and Niarchos.

Eugenie's final breakdown had been caused by her discovery that

Stavros intended to invite his four-year-old daughter, Elena Anne, and her mother to the island that summer. Elena had been conceived in a strange interlude in 1965 when he married Charlotte Ford, daughter of Henry, in a Juarez motel suite two days after Eugenie had divorced him on the grounds of incompatibility. It was a shotgun wedding (Henry Ford pointed both barrels at Stavros's head when he learned that his daughter was having his baby). Two years later, after Charlotte had returned to the same town and divorced Stavros, he went back to Eugenie and their four children.

On the surface, Eugenie remained calm and dignified throughout this entire episode, and said nothing even when the Ford heiress proclaimed that she was 'the only woman Niarchos has ever loved'. But privately Eugenie was distraught, drinking heavily, and continually threatening to kill herself. (In a letter to the London *Times* on 20 May explaining the 'mystery' of the delay in summoning professional help for the dying Eugenie, a friend of Niarchos's revealed that the doctor on the nearby island was not sent for because 'it was known from previous experience' that special equipment would be required that the Spetsai doctor did not have.)

After Tina had taken the two youngest Niarchos children to stay with her in England, Christina asked Alexander to speak to Ari about his continuing attempts to keep Eugenie's death an issue. 'Tell Daddy the account's closed. The first of the line is dead,' she told her brother. 'He's only hurting little Maria and Constantine now. They've lost their mother, and all he can think about is destroying their father.'

It had been an eventful year for Christina. She had lost a fiancée, her virginity, a baby, an aunt, and her lover.

And it was still only September.

—6—

*Anything may be expected and
anything may be supposed of a
woman who is in love*

Honoré de Balzac
The Physiology of Marriage

CHRISTINA HAD SEEN QUICKER THAN ANYONE that her mother's marriage to Sunny Blandford was over. 'They're playing out injury time, and I don't think there is very much of that,' she told her brother Alexander several months before the death of aunt Eugenie. She was still very fond of 'Sunbun' and her distinguished stepfamily. She had been happy at Lee Place, the only real home she had known, and the thought of it all coming to an end was another loss in a year of losses.

It was understandable that Christina wanted to put 1970 behind her as quickly as possible, but 'that horrible, horrible year' had also brought one major change. It was the year she began to take charge of her own life. 'What have you done?' asked a friend who met her in Paris in October, conscious that something had changed in Christina and not sure what it was. 'You look different.' Christina thought for a moment, and answered: 'I'm still the same old me. With a few more memories and a lot less expectations.'

Less expectations were also what Tina had at that moment. When she married Sunny there had been the luminous prospect of becoming Duchess of Marlborough and châtelaine of Blenheim Palace, one of the grandest houses in Britain. There are twenty-six non-royal dukes in the British aristocracy and the dukedom of Marlborough, with its connection to Sir Winston Churchill and the Vanderbilts, could fairly claim to be the best known. But as she joined in the family celebrations for her father-in-law's seventy-third birthday that September, it was widely accepted that Blenheim was no longer part of her future.

In the four months since her sister's death, Tina had become closer

47

to her own family roots, and found real satisfaction in taking care of the younger Niarchoses. She had always liked Stavros, and he never made any secret of his fondness for her. Now the death in the family had brought them closer together than ever.

But Eugenie continued to cast a shadow as the year came to a close. Christmas promised to be a melancholy time that would emphasize the divisions within the two families. The Niarchos children would rejoin their father at the Villa Marguns in St Moritz. Tina and Christina would stay at the nearby Villa Bambi with uncle George, his twenty-year-old wife, Lita, their two children, Arietta and Eugenie, and grandmother Livanos. There was no mention of Sunny joining them, although James and Henrietta had been invited for part of the holiday. Ari was off some place with Jackie and her children, Caroline and John; Alexander was spending the vacation with the new woman in his life, Baroness Fiona Thyssen-Bornemisza.

Christina had loved Eugenie no less than anyone else in the family, but now she felt the mourning had to stop. It had been seven months since her aunt had died, and she wanted to get on with her life. Alexander's new-found happiness with Fiona merely served to emphasize her own dissatisfactions. 'What's the use of being called a "fun-loving heiress" if you don't have fun?' she screamed (she screamed a lot – with pleasure as well as in rage) at Alexander when he called to wish her happy Christmas.

A few days later, she met Luis Sosa Basualdo at the Corviglia Club. The nice thing about Luis was that he really did look like a polo-player. Tall and tanned with black eyes and brilliantined hair, he was attractive to women and men rather liked him too, even when they saw through the bounderish charm. An Argentinian, a friend of Danny Marentette from summers spent in Southampton, Long Island, he was lunching with Gianni Agnelli, Tina and Stavros, and a South American friend named Peter Bemberg, when Christina came over to the table.

'Hey, I know you, Luis,' she said, when they were introduced. 'You're the one who sold those crappy ponies to my friend Amanda Haynes!'

It was true that he had sold a couple of ponies to Miss Haynes, who was keen to become acquainted with the British aristocracy and seemed to believe that two polo ponies were as good as one Trojan horse. The suggestion that he had sold her two inferior ponies hurt his professional pride. That Christina pronounced his name 'Looee', as in Armstrong, upset his Latin sensibility.

'And how is Danny?' he answered pointedly, to warn her just how much he knew about *her* past. 'I hear you had a little problem in the summer. He's still very upset.'

Christina appeared to be pleased to hear it. Perhaps it was the excitement of meeting a man who knew her secrets, or perhaps it was simply Luis's apparent availability, but before she said goodbye she asked him what he was doing for dinner that evening. Would he care to come to the Villa Bambi? Basualdo said he had arranged to dine with Bemberg and another friend, Prince Rodrigue d'Aremberg, and would probably go on to the King's Club later. If she would care to join them, he invited her to call him at the Palace Hotel.

The Palace was the best hotel in town but like most things in Basualdo's glamorous young life it wasn't quite what it seemed. He was being subsidized by the hotel's proprietor, Andrea Badrutt, who liked to have attractive young people around the place. 'He gave me a room with four meals a day for something like fifteen dollars a day. I had room 16 on the *bel étage*, which was very comfortable,' Basualdo recalls the arrangement.

He had barely got back to his room when the telephone rang and Christina was on the line pressing the invitation to dine at the Villa Bambi. He could bring his friends, she said. Afterwards they would watch a movie, she added the familiar bait. Dinner was fine, the movie was *From Here to Eternity*. Christina sat close to Basualdo, squeezing his hand with some emotion as they watched Burt Lancaster make love to Deborah Kerr on a beach at night. Afterwards they went to the King's Club and danced until it was light in the streets. 'I took her home in a taxi which cost me thirty Swiss francs,' says Basualdo, with his excellent memory for detail. 'I didn't even kiss her goodnight.'

Life in St Moritz at holiday time has a relentless rhythm to it, a sense of some predestined purpose. And after three days of skiing with Christina, three days of lunching with her at the Corviglia Club, and as many nights dining with her, and dancing with her at the King's Club until 5 a.m., it was sufficiently apparent that Luis Sosa Basualdo was soon to find out what that purpose was.

The relationship had already reached a level at which confidences as well as life stories were exchanged. Christina now knew that Luis had been born and brought up in Buenos Aires, had a small inheritance of $70,000 from his parents – his father, Lieutenant-Colonel Hector Basualdo, had married Countess Amanda Theresa Bissone-Facio de Arias, a member of a notable family. Playing polo in Palm Beach in 1966, when he was just twenty years old, he was discovered by John Coleman, an immensely rich scientist and polo patron, who signed him for his team Radiation (after his New York company, Radiation Research) to play the summer season in England. It turned out to be a perfect way to gatecrash English society: Prince Philip had his own team; Prince Charles was learning the game; every team he played was a mixture of wealthy aristocrats (like Lord Vestey, whose family owned vast tracts of land in Argentina, breeding beef for their Dewhurst butchers chain) and professionals. As his handicap rose to six (the highest is ten), Luis found no shortage of patrons in England and France. He was soon to sign a deal with Alberto Darbovan ('the coffee king of Hamburg') for $2,500 a month, plus a car and accommodation. In March he was to return to Argentina to choose a string of ponies and ship them to Hanover, Darbovan's team base.

Christina knew all this by the third day, but one detail in particular stayed in her mind. Luis had a lover. For three years, he had told her, he had been having an affair with a girl named Justine Cushing, a beautiful New York socialite, whom he was due to meet in a few days' time in the Austrian ski resort of St Anton.

Christina's deep affection for Basualdo, and even deeper disconsolation at his imminent departure for St Anton, were soon matters of common gossip in the bars and clubs of St Moritz. Basualdo was not a wealthy man; that he was about to walk out on one of the world's greatest heiresses was the stuff of romantic legend. Peppo Vannini, who ran the King's Club, and was living with the English actress Victoria Tennent, could not believe his friend Basualdo's foolhardiness. 'He said to me, "Gaucho" – he always called me Gaucho – "Gaucho, you cannot leave *Christina Onassis*! She's so *fond* of you. She's so *keen* on you. *This is Christina Onassis!* You cannot do this!" But I was more romantic than I am now and I said I didn't care and I was leaving for St Anton in the morning,' Basualdo remembers the scene.

Christina's last night with Basualdo at the King's Club was an emotional and difficult time. 'She was becoming very melodramatic, saying: "I'm going to miss you, Luis. When are you coming back? Please

come back to me." I said I would think about it, but I really intended
to go back to New York with Justine. I was going to marry her, I
thought,' says Basualdo, who was nevertheless gratified at the susceptibility he had touched off in Christina in their brief acquaintance.

At 2 a.m., when Luis announced that he needed an early night – he
had to be up early to catch the train to St Anton – Christina offered to
help him pack. (Whether she had ever packed a suitcase in her life is a
moot point.) To avoid an emotional farewell scene in the club, he
accepted the offer and took her back to room 16 of the Palace Hotel.
But as he took out his suitcase and began emptying the wardrobe and
drawers, Christina climbed on to his bed and closed her eyes.

She had not undressed. It seemed clear to Luis that she was feigning
sleep. In repose, 'she had a beautiful face, nice bone structure.' He liked
her thin delicate arms, her beautiful hands, and clear olive skin. She had
a full bosom, not too large; although her thighs were a little heavy, her
ankles and calves were fine.

'I got the message,' he recalled the moment when he began making
love to her for the first time.

'Oh no, Luis, you mustn't,' she protested as he removed her last piece
of underwear. 'If you do it, my father will say I'm a whore. We mustn't.'

'Danny made love to you and got you pregnant,' he reminded her
gently.

Her answer still puzzles Basualdo.

'She said, "What do you mean? That was like an immaculate concep-
tion." I said, "Tell me another one." She said, "No, I never had anything
to do with Danny. I'm a virgin." I said, "Sure, and pigs might fly." It
was a weird conversation, actually,' he says.

When they stopped talking, Luis discovered that although she was
certainly not virginal, she was not very experienced either. 'Luis, Luis,'
he recalls her shocked cries of pleasure. 'What are you doing to me? I'm
fainting, I'm fainting.'

At 5. a.m., he took her home in a taxi. She said she was stunned,
stunned: 'You've screwed me silly, Luis,' she told him over and over.

Luis could not have been thinking too straight either when he gave
her his telephone number in St Anton.

She began calling him as soon as he arrived at his Austrian love-nest.
And given Christina's persistence and Basualdo's needs, it was inevitable
that her calls and his moments of fulfilment would often coalesce,

making Miss Cushing very angry indeed.

Justine, whose father, Alexander Cushing, owned Squaw Valley, sometime venue of the Winter Olympics, was not only the love of Basualdo's life but quite a catch in her own right. Basualdo was devastated when she gave him the ultimatum: that heiress or this heiress. After careful consideration, he returned to that heiress in St Moritz. 'The pressure of Christina's calls and my intrinsic ambition caused me to ruin my relationship with Justine and drew me back to St Moritz like a magnet,' he now describes the dilemma he faced in January 1970.

Christina could not believe her luck. Basualdo was a tireless lover as well as an educative one. In the following weeks their lives fell into an immutable pattern of lovemaking and socializing. At 11 a.m. each morning she collected him at the Palace Hotel to begin a morning's skiing before lunch at the Corviglia with her family and friends. At 3.30 p.m. she returned to the villa to bath and change before returning to Luis's room at 4.15 p.m. 'If she was any later, I told her I would leave her. She was always punctual,' Basualdo recalls fondly. 'Between 4.15 and 6.30 we made love. Then she would go back to the villa and I would swim in the hotel pool until 7.30, have a massage, then get ready to meet her at nine in the bar, or at Niarchos's or Livanos's villa.' After the *de rigueur* stint at King's, she would spend the night in room 16. 'I would take her home at about six in the morning in a taxi, which cost thirty Swiss francs every time. It was very expensive.'

The circumstances which evoked this final *cri de coeur* were soon to surface in St Moritz. As Basualdo's relationship with the heiress grew, and his hold over her strengthened, his gallantry waned. Although he stopped accompanying her back to the Villa Bambi at dawn, Christina continued to ask for the thirty francs to pay the cab fare. Basualdo was not a wealthy man, and paying for lovers' transport was not a thing he was accustomed to doing.

Matters came to a head in the middle of February. Basualdo was feeling especially strapped after a dinner at the Villa Bambi, listening to a night of high financial table talk as removed from his comprehension as Newtonian physics. Christina had gone on and on about the number of ships her father had, and how many her mother and uncle George had. 'She made me feel poor. I was poor anyway.' When she nudged him awake at 6 a.m. and asked for her cab fare home he could stand it no longer. 'Listen, you've got so many fucking ships, pay your own fucking taxi fare!' he yelled at her, then turned over and went back to sleep. She never asked for the taxi fare again.

But Basualdo quickly made up for his unkindness that night. In the third week of February the Corviglia Club held its annual contest to elect the season's beauty queen. Although it was a light-hearted affair, with beauties like Victoria Tennent and George's wife Lita (known as the Child Bride) in the running, it was also a contest that was watched with keen interest. Basualdo lobbied furiously behind the scenes for Christina, and rather against the odds she carried off the crown.

Christina had shown, first with Danny Marentette, and now with Luis Basualdo, that she liked her men to take a strong line with her. It was something Tina understood very well ('Sunny was too *nice*,' she admitted to a friend in London), and realized that her daughter was sleeping with Basualdo some time before Christina admitted it. 'I knew you were having an affair when I noticed you were bringing your stockings home in your purse,' she said when Christina told her about her visits to the Palace Hotel. 'And I knew it had to be Luis when he started ordering you around in front of people.'

Tina's tolerance towards her daughter's affair was not altogether an acceptance of Christina's womanhood. In the sexual heat of St Moritz, Tina had started an affair of her own – with her brother-in-law, Eugenie's widower, Stavros Niarchos. She was grateful for her daughter's preoccupation with *her* lover at such a delicate moment. For while they had been able to hide their affair from the press and even from close friends – Stavros had installed Doris, the former Mrs Yul Brynner, in his chalet as a 'beard' – it might have been harder to keep it from Christina.

Only one thing troubled Tina. Christina was taking no precautions with Luis, and neither was he. 'Are you crazy, after what happened with Danny Marentette last year?' she exploded. 'He's a Catholic,' Christina said, as if that explained everything.

'In those days, Christina was *very* confused,' says Basualdo. 'She wanted to marry me. She wanted to elope. I thought about it. But she was totally dependent. I told her. "Look, you've got a place in London, $4,000 a month, and that's it. If you elope you'll be cut off. What I'm being paid to play polo is not enough to live the way you want to live."'

At the beginning of March, the season nearly over, his funds almost gone, Basualdo prepared to leave for Argentina to buy the polo ponies for his patron in Germany. Christina begged him not to go. 'If you leave now, we'll never see each other again.' When that thought failed to convince him, she tried the jealousy tactic: Mick Flick (heir with his younger brother Muck to the Mercedes-Benz fortune) had been calling her for weeks asking for a date. But Basualdo was not impressed. 'Go out with whoever you want,' he told her, intending to do the same. (He had plans to revisit Lucy Pearson, the daughter of Viscount Cowdray, of whom he had grown quite fond during his last trip to England.)

Both furious with Basualdo for leaving her, yet missing their lovemaking dreadfully, she called Mick Flick in Paris and invited him to dinner. They got on famously – as dinner companions. There was one problem. Mick confessed that only blondes turned him on. Christina became a blonde. But when they made love it still wasn't right for Mick. 'He didn't like my black bush,' she told a later lover. 'So I became a blonde down there, too.' It still did nothing for Mick, who was beginning to wish he hadn't encouraged her in the first place. But Christina was not deterred. Mick felt compelled to flee her overtures.

Seven o'clock one morning, several months after his first dinner date with Christina, Flick telephoned Ari's right-hand man in New York and asked if he could call by and talk to him before he caught the morning flight to Germany. Flick came straight to the point when he arrived at Johnny Meyer's hotel an hour later. He had been dating Christina, he said, and he liked and respected her, but he didn't want to get married until he was forty-five – and he had about eight years to go. 'Would you tell Mr Onassis that for me?' he asked Meyer. 'Tell him I respect him and I respect his family, but I don't want to get married yet.'

Alexander had a theory about his little sister. Her erratic behaviour in the past twelve months – the affair with Danny Marentette, the abortion, her fling with the unsuitable Luis Basualdo, her public pursuit of Mick Flick – were Christina's attempts to concentrate their father's mind on her 'at any cost,' he claimed. 'She had mixed feelings about our father, everybody did, but she still craved his attention, she still wanted his blessing.'

It was true that Jackie, Ari's new wife, had been occupying a great deal of his attention, trespassing on Christina's territory. It had been a long time since he called his daughter *Chryso mou* – his golden one – and she was feeling neglected, if not abandoned.

As she travelled alone to Monte Carlo at the beginning of May, knowing that her mother was about to start divorce proceedings against Sunny (on grounds of irretrievable breakdown of the marriage), Christina was in a reflective mood. She knew that she had withdrawn from close contact with the rest of the family. For the moment she had no lover, not even a close girlfriend in her life. She had no career, and no ideas about finding one. 'I knew I had come to the end of some road,' she later admitted. 'I just wanted to get my life back on track.'

She stayed on the *Christina*. But without other guests, without her father to bring it alive, the yacht had no magic for her. She wandered up to the Hôtel de Paris to see who was in town. She met Rodney Solomon, who had been a regular weekend guest at Lee Place. They sat and talked by the swimming pool. After a while, a friendly American joined them. He was in town for the convention of the Young Presidents Organization, he told them. In her direct way, Christina asked: How old are you? He said he was forty-eight, and that was still young – 'for a president'. She was surprised when he told her his age. He looked younger than that. His grey hair was tousled; his body still taut. He had a soft West Coast accent. They talked about skiing and tennis. His name was Joe. When they met the following day, they sat together and talked some more. He told her about his interests, the organizations he belonged to (Los Angeles Beautiful Committee; American Friends of the Israel Museum; Americans for Change; Republican Task Force; the Navy League). She thought there was something very vulnerable about a man who joined so much. He invited kindness, and when he was leaving the following morning, returning to Los Angeles via Frankfurt and London, she asked him to call her when he got to London: 'if you have the time'. She wrote her name and number in her Filofax. It was not until she tore out the page and handed it to him that he realized who she was. ('Oh *that* Christina,' he said. 'Yeah, *that* one,' she smiled, always pleased to be recognized.) Ten days later Joseph Bolker called from Germany and asked her to dinner.

He invited another couple to join them, and would later remember their first evening together as 'fun, very amusing – she was a bright, attractive, interesting personality'. She liked him more and more. He was at least ten years older than any man she had ever dated before, and she liked his maturity, the 'quiet way he controls things'. It also struck her that there was the same age difference between them as there was between her mother and father (twenty-nine years). It didn't worry her that he had been married before (to Home Savings and Loan heiress Janice Taper) and had four daughters close to her own age. 'She saw Joe as her link to the adult world,' said Ari's aide Johnny Meyer. Describing Bolker to a friend shortly after their first date, she said: 'He's charming and smart ... he's a dinky millionaire in real estate.'

When Bolker flew back to Los Angeles, Christina went out to the airport to say goodbye. They were not yet lovers, but at Heathrow she pressed him, in a manner that was unmistakably an invitation to put their relationship on to an intimate basis, to come back as soon as possible. He returned to Europe three times between the end of May and the middle of July. They met in Paris and London and spent weekends in small out-of-the-way hotels on the south coast of England. Between their rendezvous she wrote him daily letters (in handwriting that Bolker called 'early high-school period') and telephoned him every morning at ten o'clock when she woke in London, ignoring the fact that it was 2 a.m. in Los Angeles.

Joseph Bolker, at first enchanted with her directness, and amused by her openness about her life and her feelings, was beginning to become uneasy. He expected her to moderate her behaviour as the weeks went by; it was a familiar pattern in such affairs. Instead, Christina was showing signs of a fatal attraction; what at first had been vaguely endearing was becoming vaguely threatening. He tried to cool it, cancelled his next trip to London, wasn't available when she called. It only made matters worse. Her letters now became long, passionate cables, her morning telephone call was repeated a dozen times throughout the day and night. Bolker's first sense of satisfaction that a girl of twenty should fancy him so much was forgotten as she continued to increase the pressure.

He tried to make allowances. He knew that she was deeply troubled by the recent rapid decline in her relationship with her father, who had flown into a rage when he got the message from Mick Flick. 'You're making a mockery of the Onassis name,' he yelled at her on the telephone. Ari always found surprising ways to underline his disapproval of her behaviour: ten days after he had given her an emerald bracelet and necklace worth $300,000, he refused to pay for a television set she had bought for her bedroom when she had the flu. Sobbing and bemused,

Christina called Bolker in Los Angeles: 'I don't understand, Joe. What is he doing to me?'

It is unlikely that Joseph Bolker's attempt to help her understand her father's motives eased Christina's mind. 'Christina, it's obvious, the television set only the maid sees, or whoever you invite into your bedroom,' he told her. 'But when you wear those jewels the whole world sees them, they reflect on *his* wealth and on *his* image, and that's why he does those things.'

Bolker had no time for Ari. 'He used his children, his family, he used everybody: he would publicly say, "I love my daughter, I love my son," but there was no love, he had no feelings, no conscience, he was a user of everybody,' he said. And in spite of his fears about the way his affair with Christina was going, in spite of the stress she was placing on his own nervous system, and the aggressiveness of her mood swings, he still wanted to help her.

This happened in 1971, in the month of July. She turned up on his doorstep unannounced in Los Angeles. She had an expression of distress which was accentuated by the pallor of travel in her face. Her thick, smooth as glass, shoulder-length hair had reverted to its natural black ('black as a raven's wing,' Ari liked to describe it). There was something about her whole appearance that spelled trouble to Joseph Bolker as soon as he opened the door.

'Does your mother know you're here?' was the first question he asked. Christina admitted that she didn't. He dialled Tina himself in the South of France. 'Believe me, this is none of my doing,' he said after he had explained what had happened.

Joseph Bolker's large modern apartment on the twenty-fourth floor of Century Towers West was a bachelor's dream. A neurotic teenager (even if her name was Christina Onassis and her father was one of the richest men in the world) was the last person he wanted hanging out there. He didn't say this exactly, not in as many words, but that is what was in his mind as he talked to the marchioness at Mas de la Rue. He felt he couldn't make himself clearer. He knew that Christina was listening on the bedroom extension, saying nothing at all, and he was addressing her as much as he was speaking to her mother.

'We do have a problem,' Tina conceded in her measured English voice after showing a moment's surprise. 'I certainly do not want my daughter living with a man she isn't married to.'

That is what Bolker expected her to say. Only he had miscalculated her feelings concerning her daughter, and his sense of relief was shortlived.

'She must return to England at once,' Tina continued. 'Or make it legal.'

Bolker protested to Tina that he didn't *want* to marry Christina. And even if he did, he said, Ari would never permit it.

Tina reminded Bolker that Christina loved him very much ... but if he cared so little about her feelings, then he should send her home at once. She then politely, *chillingly* asked him to put down his receiver – 'because I don't want to hang up on you, Mr Bolker,' she said.

Christina, who had heard every word, 'began to yell even before she came out of the bedroom,' Bolker recalled later. 'What's *wrong* with me? Why *won't* you marry me? Aren't I *good enough* for you?' she screamed at him for maybe an hour. Then suddenly she seemed to calm down, and returned to the bedroom. Bolker stayed in the living room. He felt in a state of shock. Her paranoid outburst had drained everything out of him. He closed his eyes, perhaps he dozed for a few moments.

When he woke he became aware of a sense of silence from the bedroom. 'I didn't hear any sounds, so I went in and she was lying there. She had taken some pills. I thought, "Oh my God, what have you done?" There was a young doctor in the condominium across the hall, and I went and grabbed him. He started walking her around and pouring liquids down her and finally brought her round.'

Christina's first words scared Bolker all over again.

'I am going to go on doing this until you marry me,' she promised.

'I guess if you feel that strongly about it,' he told her, 'we'll get married.'

It wasn't, Joseph Bolker admitted later, the most eager proposal of marriage he had ever made in his life.

————

The civil ceremony took place in Las Vegas on 27 July. Ari was celebrating Jackie's forty-second birthday on Skorpios when he got the news. The first person he saw was Johnny Meyer, who remembered: 'He was acting like a crazy man.' It was a day, said Meyer, he never wanted to go through again. Ari knew all about Joseph Bolker, of course. According to the reliable Meyer, 'Ari had a file on Bolker before

Bolker had finished his soup on his very first date with Christina.' Ari had also been bugging Christina's London mews flat for some time and knew how dependent on the American his daughter was becoming. But the idea that she would actually want to marry him had not crossed his mind. And although some people saw this as a measure of the distance that had come between Ari and Christina, *nobody* had expected it.

Luis Basualdo was in Hamburg when he read about the marriage in Las Vegas in German newspapers. 'I was shocked, shed some tears. I called her. She said, "Luis, if you try to get in touch with me again, after all you've done to me, I will call the police. When you left me you broke my heart." So I didn't call again. I used to cry myself to sleep in Hamburg,' he admitted later. Why did she marry Joseph Bolker? 'She did it to escape, to get even with her family, to be the centre of attention,' said Basualdo.

And so while Christina was starting life in California as the third Mrs Joseph Bolker, Ari on his island was plotting to destroy even the very small chance of success that extraordinary marriage had. Bolker was his target, his new *bête noire*. Bolker had taken over from Niarchos as his private enemy number one. 'This guy has made a fortune marrying heiresses,' Ari said unreasonably (reason had nothing to do with it when Ari was in a rage). 'I'm going to make him wish this time he'd peddled his stinking fish in some other street.'

Christina knew her father well enough to know that he could not ignore what she had done. And while she waited for the inevitable backlash from Skorpios – 'it was like waiting for the other Gucci to drop,' she later told Alexander – she gave small dinner parties for Joe's friends (Zsa Zsa Gabor was a frequent guest; Nicky Haslam, a British interior decorator, remembers Christina being 'rather spaced out' most of the time), played tennis, surfed, walked on the beach. 'The ocean air is healing,' she told Joe, who shared her pain, who understood how deeply she felt her father's disapproval, and who saw through her bravado. 'The ocean air is life to a Greek,' she said.

In spite of the ill-omened start to the marriage, and some early faint signs that her unspectacular lifestyle was beginning to chafe (her telephone calls to friends in Paris, catching up on all the gossip, increased alarmingly, remembered Bolker, who got the bills), there was an inescapable tenderness about their early days as man and wife. 'We enjoyed sleeping together and talking to each other and everything was good.

We satisfied each other's needs,' Bolker remembered how it was. But in a gesture that seemed symbolic, she had her husband diving into the surf at La Jolla for hours when her wedding ring was washed off her finger. 'She was very distressed,' said Bolker. 'We both knew it was hopeless, but she didn't want to give up.'

Still busy clearing the way for his revenge, Ari secretly admired what his daughter had done. There was no value in obedience if you didn't have it in you to rebel once in a while. Nevertheless, she had to be taught a lesson. In December she would be twenty-one and due to collect $75 million from her trust fund. Ari rewrote the terms, postponing her access to the fortune that would set her free. 'Tell her as long as she is married to that man she doesn't collect a nickel,' he told Johnny Meyer, who was ordered to California to talk to the Bolkers.

Christina had known Meyer all her life. She liked him, but she also knew that behind his funny charm he was a ruthless emissary of her father's will. He was 'capable of having people assassinated, having your legs broken or something. Christina said that he did a lot of things for her father, he took care of a lot of situations for him,' Bolker later told Peter Evans.

The trio met for lunch in the Polo Lounge at the Beverly Hills Hotel. Meyer outlined the world according to Aristotle Onassis. He emphasized Ari's total and unyielding disapproval of the marriage, his 'deep hurt' at learning about it only after the ceremony had taken place. Christina expressed her own 'deep hurt' on learning that she was to be denied access to her own trust fund. 'The money's yours the day you divorce Joe,' Meyer told her. Listening to this, Bolker stayed calm. He was capable of supporting his own wife, he told Meyer with a dignity that suggested none of the apprehensions and fragility with which he had entered that wedlock.

Perhaps sensing a loyalty in Bolker that would not easily be resolved, Meyer moved on to 'the serious implications' the marriage might have on Ari's business interests. 'You see, Joe, Ari has a lot of dealings with the Saudis. Maybe they won't like the idea of a Jew in the family. If they pulled their contracts, the banks could get nervous. Nervous banks are bad news. It'd do more than scrape the paintwork if they called in their loans.' It was a line Joe Bolker had been expecting; Christina had warned him that her father had anti-Semitic tendencies in his personal dealings. He had plenty of Saudi friends, Bolker answered, and he had no cause whatsoever to believe that any of them harboured animosity towards Jewish Americans.

Christina and Joe agreed that the lunch had worked out better than they had expected. Meyer seemed genuinely sympathetic to their cause. When they said goodbye that afternoon at the Beverly Hills Hotel, he promised that he would try to get Ari to see their side of the story. 'We felt that he understood the situation, that we had a friend,' Bolker recalled. But their hopes were quickly dashed.

Bolker was not prepared for the sheer totality of Ari's displeasure when it began a few days after Johnny Meyer returned to Paris (ignoring his promise, Meyer gave a completely negative report on the Bolkers to Ari). 'The moment I left for the office in the morning Christina started to get telephone calls from people trying to talk her into getting a divorce, telling her things about me, all kinds of incredible and dumb and untrue things, anything to discredit me.' Stories implicating Bolker with organized crime began to spread in Los Angeles and New York, then in London and Paris. (Typical of the stories suddenly surfacing in US tabloid newspapers was the suggestion that he was the front man for a mob company selling gambling equipment to casinos in Europe and the Far East.) Each day brought some further accusation, some new drama. 'When a billion dollars leans on you, you feel it,' he was supposed to have said afterwards, and although he didn't recall ever putting it in those exact words it was clear to him that Ari was 'systematically nullifying' him, his business and his marriage. 'I would go home and Christina would be so distraught. Like somebody had called and said I was a member of the Mafia. After a while it just wore her down,' Joseph Bolker recalled later.

As unhappy as she had ever been in her life, in a continual state of unrest, and thoroughly frightened, Christina called her mother in New York. To Bolker's surprise, Tina urged her daughter to come and see her at once. Christina caught the afternoon TWA flight to Kennedy International. They met in Tina's suite at the Regency Hotel on Park Avenue. It was still less than five weeks after the wedding in Las Vegas. Christina said, 'I'm just trying to work out a life I can live with. Doesn't Daddy want me to be happy?' Entirely sympathetic and unusually perceptive, Tina told Christina not to listen to the stories about Joe, which were simply Ari's way of testing her faith in her new husband as well as her conviction in the marriage. 'You must prove to him that you're right and he's wrong.' It was a game of nerves which Christina had to win, Tina explained. To help make her feel better, and to compensate for the untouchable trust fund, she secretly gave her daughter a cheque for $200,000 to buy a beach house in California.

It was a brilliant stroke. Now set to marry Niarchos as soon as she had shed the marquess, the money was both a way of buying Christina's understanding, or at least her neutrality (probably the most she could hope for in the circumstances), and also encourage her daughter to stay put in California with the man Ari hated most in all the world. Keeping the Christina crisis going on the West Coast was the surest way Tina knew to divert Ari's attention from what she was up to in Europe.

On 22 October, five weeks after the summit meeting in New York, eighteen months after Eugenie's death on Spetsopoula, Tina and Stavros Niarchos were wed in Paris. Christina got the news from the message operator at Century Towers. Bolker had to 'practically tie her down' when she realized how cunningly and completely she had been duped by her mother. 'It was a very emotional time, a lot of yelling and screaming, a really bad scene,' Bolker later recalled.

In *Ari*, Evans wrote: 'Tina was smart of course, and selfish, and on the evidence she was more hard-boiled than anyone had ever thought possible, including Ari. The marriage had shaken him every bit as profoundly as it had Christina. It was not, as he later said so often, "that the grave had hardly closed on her sister and Niarchos's wife," that upset him so much, but that he still regarded Tina, a decade and two marriages after their divorce, as his wife – she was and ever must be his wife, and wife absolutely, and wife eternally: she was the mother of his children.'

Christina understood this in her bones. She was certain that Niarchos had married her mother to revenge himself on her father. And it would not stop there. She told Bolker, 'Stavros killed Eugenie and he's going to kill my mother.' If there was a moment when Joseph Bolker knew that his marriage to Christina was over it was the moment he learned that Tina had married Stavros Niarchos. 'It was the one thing that would bring Christina and her father together again. It was only a matter of time before Christina gave me the hard word,' he later recalled.

Christina took a ritual overdose a few days after receiving the news from Paris, but recovered sufficiently to fly alone to London at the beginning of November. In Los Angeles, Bolker issued a statement claiming that at his suggestion she had gone to London 'to see her doctor ... and hopefully to resolve family problems'. (Privately he added, 'And I'm a big part of the problem.')

In London, Christina opened her heart to Fiona Thyssen, her brother's mistress. Joe was a decent and honourable man and they were genuinely fond of each other, Christina said, but even without the pressure coming from Ari, they both knew that the marriage had been a bad mistake. 'And it's my mistake,' Christina admitted the part she had played in forcing the wedding on Bolker. 'It's entirely my fault, and I don't want to hurt Joe any more.'

The situation was more serious than Christina realized.

Fiona had recently found a transcript on her desk in Belgravia. Imagining that it belonged to Alexander (they had no secrets between them), she read it. It was a transcript of a conversation between Johnny Meyer and another Onassis executive. The transcript (inadvertently left behind by a friend of Alexander's, an Onassis chieftain) made it clear that Ari intended 'to do a number on Bolker, he wanted to hurt the fellow, not do him in, but certainly do him harm in some way,' she later recalled.

Unless Christina moved fast, Fiona knew that Bolker was going to get badly hurt – simply because he had been nice enough to allow himself to be railroaded by Tina into a marriage for her own dubious ends.

'You don't want to be married to Joe. He doesn't want to be married to you,' Fiona told Christina. 'There is no question of anybody ripping anybody off. Go back to California on the first plane tomorrow, tell Joe that you want a divorce, and in a few weeks it will be all over and nobody need be involved except you and Joe.'

It was good advice and Christina was smart enough to take it.

She returned to California in time for the party Bolker had arranged at the Bistro in Beverly Hills for her twenty-first birthday. 'I had to get away for a little time to deal with my feelings,' she told a friend. 'I needed to come to terms with myself.'

As lawyers began quietly unravelling the marriage, Christina and Joe went on one last holiday together, skiing in California's Sun Valley in the second week of January. But she fell on the first day and dislocated her shoulder. Ari sent her a crate of Greek olives – still on their branches. 'It was a nice touch,' admitted Bolker.

On 3 February 1972, seven months after the Las Vegas nuptials, it was officially announced that the marriage was over. Unaware of Fiona's intervention, convinced that it was all his doing, Ari made no secret of his satisfaction and sense of victory. To make sure that Bolker and everybody else knew that it was his wish and all his work, he sent Meyer and two armed heavies to escort Christina back to New York. (It was quite a performance: the captain refused to take off until they handed over their .45s.) Christina told reporters: 'Although Joe will soon be my ex-husband, he will always be my best friend.' What went wrong? 'I'm too Greek and he's too Beverly Hills,' she said.

She checked into the Regency Hotel and talked to her father in Paris. It was the first time they had spoken together since her marriage to Joseph Bolker. 'How are you, Daddy?' she asked. 'I had a mild touch of apoplexy but I'm all right now,' he told her. He called her *Chryso mou*, she would recall later, and he had not called her that for a very long time.

The following day, assured that the $75 million trust fund would soon be hers, she changed her mind about returning to London. London in February was no fun at all. She would go to Buenos Aires instead.

She knew that Luis Basualdo would be there, playing polo, and waiting for her.

—7—

*Blessed is the wooing that is not
long a-doing*

Robert Burton
The Anatomy of Melancholy

CHRISTINA RECOGNIZED TWO IMPORTANT THINGS about herself in New York: she was still a prisoner of her father's megalomania; and she was getting fat.

In California she had lived in track suits, in loose-fitting T-shirts and jeans; in California, she had increasingly indulged her taste for Coca-Cola. But it was not until she tried on the smart clothes she collected from the apartment at the Pierre that she realized how overweight she had become.

She delayed her trip to Buenos Aires to buy herself a whole new wardrobe. Then she decided first to fly down to Rio de Janeiro for Carnival. She was sure that with three days in the heat and relentless partying of Carnival she would quickly get back into shape for Luis Basualdo.

The idea of a reunion with Basualdo, the man who had sexually awakened her, and could always excite her even when he treated her badly, the idea of seeing him again gave back an edge to her life.

In Rio, she checked into the Copacabaña Palace, an elegant pre-war hotel on the famous beach. She planned to stay three days, leaving immediately after Carnival ended on Ash Wednesday, 16 February. The first night she met up with Ronaldo de Lima, one of the best-known polo players in Brazil. He introduced her to another polo celebrity, Paolo Fernando Marcondes-Ferraz. The rhythmic samba of Carnival is not the music of caution or prolonged courtship; they became lovers accordingly. ('We fell in love in the spirit of Rio,' Christina later told a girlfriend in New York.)

Paolo was good for her in another way too. He introduced her to a grapefruit diet, much favoured by polo players at that time. Ten days later the diet and the affair crossed the finishing line together when Christina, fifteen pounds lighter, and a great deal happier, decided to resume her journey to Buenos Aires – and Luis Basualdo.

Buenos Aires seemed very sedate after Rio. The most sophisticated and European city in South America had a sense of portent and *déjà vu* with talk of the ageing Perón and his second wife, Isabel, who were in exile in Madrid, making a political comeback to the republic he had bankrupted in the 1950s. None of this interested Christina, who regarded politics as a big yawn and had never even registered to vote in any of the countries she could call home. Growing a little bored with hotel life, she stayed with her friend Marina at the Tchomlekdjoglous' apartment on Calle Quintana.

But she could not wait to see Basualdo again and as soon as she could – no matter that it was 3 a.m. – she went to the address Marina had given her. Luis had returned moments before with a girlfriend from the Mau Mau club and was in no mood to play host to Mrs Bolker – the name she had given to the concierge. 'Tell her I'm not at home and to leave a message,' Basualdo said with satisfaction.

She returned at noon the following day. 'Luis, Luis, long time no see. Let's have lunch,' she said, ignoring their last conversation when she had threatened to call the police if he ever tried to contact her again.

They lunched at the Café La Biela. They had not seen each other for eleven months and had plenty of catching up to do. It was a Friday and Luis was due to leave for a weekend polo tournament at Rancho El Tata in Juinin. 'Listen,' he had an idea. 'Why don't you come with me? You'll love it.' It was the kind of invitation Christina loved best. 'Let me grab a few things from Marina's and you're on,' she told him, leaving the restaurant as soon as the decision was made.

On the three-hour journey she regained her old confessional closeness to Luis, telling him in quite the frankest detail about her marriage to Joseph Bolker, its problems as well as its early-day raptures. It began with sex and ended in friendship, she said, but there was no real love at all. She told him all about Mick Flick, and the trouble she had gone to in order to arouse his interest in her body. ('Blondes don't always have more fun, Luis,' she concluded sadly.)

The confidences inevitably soon came closer to home.

'She said, "Luis, I do love you but I have to admit that I had a little affair with someone else on my way here." She told me all about Paolo Fernando Marcondes-Ferraz. She also told me about the grapefruit diet,' Basualdo later remembered her fondness for random confession.

He was surprised by the ease and alacrity with which she had gone to bed with Paolo, but sexual opportunism in a woman had its attractions too. He was not angry when that weekend she let him see that she had eyes for handsome polo players like Luis Maguire and Rory Donovan. But if her behaviour was meant to tell Basualdo something new about herself, it also told him that their relationship would never be the same again. His thoughts drifted back to Lucy Pearson, Lord Cowdray's interesting daughter.

But it had been a wonderful weekend. They made love with a keenness and frequency that had not lessened one bit since St Moritz. With so little else on their minds, it came as a shock to find reporters and photographers waiting for them outside Marina's apartment on their return to Buenos Aires. 'How the hell do they know I'm here?' asked Christina, who had travelled anonymously (as Mrs Bolker) and had not even checked into a hotel.

It turned out that when they left La Biela posthaste she left behind her purse containing $20,000 in cash. The waiter handed it to the police, an act of such blinding honesty that he had become a local hero. 'The press got hold of the story and tracked Christina down to Marina's. She didn't even know she had lost the wallet,' Basualdo remembered the incident which put him and Christina on the front pages in Argentina for a week.

When the time came for Basualdo to return to New York, Christina took off for Paris to catch up with her father. 'I think he needs me,' she told Luis, although how she expected to be of help to Ari in his present difficulties she did not explain.

It was no longer a secret that his marriage to Jackie was in considerable crisis. He never tried to hide the fact that he was seeing Maria Callas again. But Jackie was not going without a struggle. The evening after he had been photographed dining at Maxim's with Callas, Jackie flew in from New York to be photographed at his side in the same restaurant. A few nights after that, Callas was admitted to the American Hospital at Neuilly suffering from an overdose. Ari made amends the following month, when Maria joined him on Tragonisis (the private island of the

Embiricos clan), with a gift of earrings and a passionate kiss on the mouth – snapped by a paparazzo. Jackie's revenge was what Christina called her 'no room at the inn strategy': more and more on his visits to New York, Ari found that he was unable to stay at his wife's apartment on Fifth Avenue: the decorators are in, Jackie would apologize, and send him packing to his permanent suite at the Pierre.

Christina watched these games with quiet amusement. She rather enjoyed her father's tribulations as he found himself bounced between his cool American wife and his fiery Greek mistress. 'It's one of God's little jests ... to pay him back for the way he's treated us,' she told Alexander. And when Alexander suggested that she was mellowing towards Jackie, Christina said: 'I don't dislike her, you know. I hate her.'

From Paris Christina telephoned Basualdo in New York several times. But his mind was now so firmly set on Lucy Pearson (and on the heavy responsibilities her father's 75,000 acres, merchant bank, newspaper chain and china factory undoubtedly would one day bring) that he could not keep the preoccupation out of his voice. 'You can't depend on polo-players,' Christina told a girlfriend in Paris. Henceforth she made it plain she was footloose and fancy free.

She embarked on a round of nightclubbing in London and Paris and New York with the likes of Arnaud de Rosnay, a young baron whose fortune came from an Indian Ocean island, and Patrick Gillis, a young skier whose fame came from an affair with Brigitte Bardot. But Mick Flick continued to fascinate her most. His earnest disinclination to go to bed with her became an open secret because Christina herself could talk of nothing else the moment Flick's name came up. ('Why won't he screw me? Rich girls need it too,' was a familiar line of hers; she knew it made people laugh.)

If she learned that a girl had slept with Flick she would call her up and demand to be told the most intimate details. Florence Grinda, a well-connected Parisian socialite, was able occasionally, and quite mischievously, to supply the name of Flick's latest conquest. 'Christina would call the poor girl immediately,' Florence later recalled. 'She wanted to know *everything*. I would say, "Christina, really have you no shame!" She would say, "Yes, yes, but I have to *know*!" She thought it was a great joke.'

At the beginning of January 1973, Christina and Alexander were told by their father that he had decided to divorce Jackie: 'My New Year's gift to you both,' was how he put it; he had a shrewd appreciation of how much it meant to them. He had consulted his lawyers in Athens, and was talking to Roy Cohn in New York. A lawyer renowned as a legal executioner (*Esquire* magazine called him 'the toughest, meanest, vilest, and one of the most brilliant lawyers in America'), it was no coincidence that Cohn was also known to be no friend of the Kennedys. 'All in all,' Ari told his daughter, 'he's the ideal man to handle this situation, wouldn't you say, *Chryso mou?*'

It was wonderful news. Christina flew off to Rio to celebrate – and to rekindle the friendships she had formed the previous year.

Alexander returned to Fiona in Switzerland, to the new house in Morges where they intended to live together. For four and a half years their affair had been a well-kept secret. But the strain on both of them had been immense and at the end of 1972, to Ari's delight, Fiona had left him. The separation was brief and only served to make them realize how much they meant to each other. As soon as the new house was ready it was decided that Alexander would resign from his father's Olympic Aviation charter company. ('It's the only way I'm going to survive,' he told Fiona. 'I can't take this grotesque man's domination for much longer.') The plan was that he would resume his studies to get the qualifications he needed to get him started in the world beyond his father's reach.

Alexander was excited about the future. He was also pleased that he had finally persuaded his father to sell their ageing Piaggio amphibian plane (a deathtrap, he said) and buy a helicopter. Ari promised that he would take the plane on one last trip to Miami in February and sell it there. Although Alexander was determined to free himself from Ari and his empire, it was good to think that his father was beginning to take notice of his ideas.

On 22 January 1973, the Onassis family by force of habit was spread around the world. Ari and Jackie were in New York. Christina was in Brazil. Tina and Stavros were in St Moritz. Fiona was in London, attending her brother's wedding. And Alexander was in Athens, where he had to check out a new American pilot for the Piaggio.

Although a seasoned amphibian pilot, Donald McCusker was not acquainted with Piaggios, and Alexander had worked out a plan to speed him through the required familiarization flying hours. 'The idea was that McCusker would be treated as a charter customer,' explained Donald McGregor, the medically grounded pilot McCusker was to replace. 'To keep it legal, Alexander [an experienced pilot] was to go with McCusker to check him out. McCusker would then "hire" the aircraft, and I would go along as dogsbody to watch how things went.' They would fly hard for a week to get McCusker's hours up before the Piaggio was ferried to Las Palmas to join the *Christina* before it sailed for Miami.

And so at 3.15 on that Monday afternoon in January, aircraft SX-BDC Piaggio 136 of Olympic Airways reached taxiway F of Athens International to hold for takeoff. Alexander was in the right-hand seat with McCusker, the pilot under supervision, on his left. McGregor took the centre passenger seat behind them. At 3.21 p.m. after Alexander had gone through the safety checks from memory (he had forgotten the preflight checklist), the Piaggio was cleared for takeoff on runway 33, with instructions to turn left when airborne.

But what happened next happened so quickly that not a single word was spoken inside the plane. Within three seconds of lift-off the right wing dropped sharply and the plane seemed to lose its balance. Strapped in the middle seat, McGregor was unable to see out but later he could remember nothing to indicate engine failure; there was no shuddering sign of a stall. 'By this time we were in a right-hand climbing turn which became quite steep,' recalled McGregor. 'I realized we were going to hit the ground.'

Ari was preparing to go to lunch at P. J. Clarke's in New York when he heard the news that his son was in surgery in Athens, undergoing an operation to remove blood clots and relieve pressure on his brain. McCusker and McGregor had also been seriously injured, he was told. He commandeered an Olympic Airways Boeing 727 and, accompanied by Jackie, returned immediately to Greece. (He also laid on a British Airways Trident to fly one man from London to Athens: the English neurosurgeon Alan Richardson.)

Tina, to whom Alexander had refused to speak a word since her marriage to the hated Stavros, was told the news while dressing for a dinner party at the Palace Hotel in St Moritz. Fiona heard the news of the accident on the radio in London, which was exactly how Christina heard about it in Rio, several hours after everybody else.

The family was still gathering at the hospital from all over the

world when Dr Richardson confirmed the Greek physicians' prognosis:
Alexander had suffered irrecoverable brain damage. Yet it still did not
seem possible. Although Alexander was on a life-support system, he
was almost completely unmarked. In repose, his face was astonishingly
young for twenty-five, he looked like a schoolboy again. His new nose,
of which he was so proud, had not been touched; a shaved patch of hair
above his right temple was the only ominous sign. Ari could not accept
that his son would not recover. A second world-class neurosurgeon was
already on his way from Boston; a sacred icon reputed to have miraculous powers was summoned from one of the islands.

It was a long vigil. The strain on everybody was immense. Ari's sisters
wept uncontrollably. Jackie appeared like a rock at Ari's side. But her
presence fooled nobody who knew what was going on in their unhappy
marriage. Jackie's thoughts behind her calm *désolée* beauty could not
help returning to her own private crisis as they waited through the night.
Noticing that Fiona was sitting alone during the small hours, she sat by
her side. She must have understood Fiona's feelings better than anyone
at that moment. After a small silence Jackie spoke in a soft voice. She
knew, she said, that Ari had discussed their forthcoming divorce with
Alexander – had he mentioned a settlement figure? Fiona was surprised
by the question, but realized it was the kind of intrusion she needed at
that moment. 'Sympathy, when you're that vulnerable, you don't need,'
she later admitted. Although Alexander knew what his father had in
mind, Fiona suggested that it was a matter Jackie should discuss directly
with her husband. Jackie agreed, and left Fiona to her thoughts.

At 1 p.m. on 23 January, the American specialist told Ari that he
could only concur with his English and Greek colleagues. Alexander
was in the deepest possible coma: he had suffered general contusion and
oedema of the brain matter; the right temporal lobe had been reduced
to pulp and the right frontal fossa severely fractured. Only the machine
was keeping Alexander technically alive. Ari told the doctors to wait
until Christina arrived from Brazil to say goodbye to her brother – 'then
let us torture him no more.'

It was the only thing he had ever done in his life as a father that Fiona
'respected on any level at all'. After Ari left the hospital to go in search
of the church in which he had prayed the night he learned of his
grandmother's death fifty years before, Fiona was permitted to sit alone
with Alexander and hold his hand for a while, trying to reach him,

trying to come to terms with the fact that 'there was no way he was going to come back from wherever he'd gone to.'

At six o'clock, Christina arrived and stayed with her brother for twenty-five minutes. They had not, for most of their lives, been close. Christina resented the way she was left on the sidelines while Alexander got all the attention as the male heir; it hurt her to know that their mother loved him more. Alexander envied Christina's freedoms; he thought she was a spoiled brat who was given everything she wanted. It was Fiona Thyssen who had 'banged their heads together' and made them recognize their mutual interests. Now they were friends and beginning to understand each other's needs and each other's anguish. Now they talked about what they might do together. But it was too late.

At 6.55 p.m., ten minutes after she had been taken weeping back to aunt Artemis's villa in Glyfada, the doctors switched off the machine that had been keeping Alexander alive – and changed Christina's life for ever.

'You are my future now,' Ari told his daughter in a choked voice the day they buried Alexander on Skorpios.

Christina stayed calm-looking on the surface that chill winter's day, but already she feared the consequences of her brother's death. Better than anyone she understood that with all the riches of the Onassis inheritance came the burden of Alexander's unfulfilled destiny.

But if Ari expected Christina to pull the sword from the stone he still did nothing to prepare her for the task. Seemingly paralysed by the aftershock of Alexander's death, he let a year go by in which Christina's new role was barely mentioned by him at all.

Convinced that the plane had been sabotaged by his enemies (the CIA, his former friend Colonel George Papadopoulos, and even McCus-ker, who with McGregor survived the accident with serious injuries, were on his list of suspects), Ari offered a million dollars for information that would confirm that his son had been murdered. For a year he could think or talk of little else. The accident investigation report, compiled by the Greek air force, seemed to confirm his suspicions. The accident, it found, had been caused because the aileron connecting cables were reversed during the installation of a new control system. Thus when the pilot, as instructed by the control tower, attempted to turn left on takeoff, the aircraft would have banked to the right; the harder he pulled the stick to the left the more sharply the plane swerved to the right. But Ari's own engineers disputed the official findings, claiming serious flaws in the investigators' procedures. Donald McCusker also dismissed the crossed-cables theory. He was convinced that the Piaggio, taking off less than two minutes behind an Air France Boeing 727, was hit by the full force of the big plane's wake vortices. The 'murder' enquiries came to nothing in the end; nobody even tried to claim the reward money.

Ari's year-long morbid preoccupation with Alexander's death gave Tina an opportunity to rebuild bridges with Christina. But Tina was seldom without some self-serving thought in her mind and, prompted by the matriarchal Arietta Livanos, she put to Christina an extraordinary proposal. It was this: Christina should marry her cousin (and Tina's stepson) Philippe Niarchos. 'You like Philippe, he likes you, why don't you two live together and see whether you can fall in love?' Tina suggested a few months after Alexander's death. 'You have my blessing and the blessing of granny Livanos and uncle Stavros.'

It was coldblooded and cruel in its sentimentality but it was also a brilliant bid to unite the divided families ∴.. and to consolidate their fortunes.

Ari was not consulted; nor, remarkably, did he discover what was going on during the summer of 1973 as Christina and Philippe tried to bring off their families' desired but improbable fantasy. The experiment was not unpleasant, Christina later confessed, but it never rose above the perfunctory coupling of old friends whose hearts were not in the grand design planned for them. 'If only they had had a little more maturity ... or a little less,' Tina later sighed away her disappointment. Timing, as Ari always told her, is everything in life.

—8—

And Agag said, Surely the
bitterness of death is past

1. Samuel xv.32

IN AUGUST, ARI RETURNED TO SKORPIOS for the first time since
Alexander's death. He knew it would be hard for him. But he did not
want the island to become a shrine, regarded only as the place where
his son was buried. 'I want to hear laughter and music there again,' he
told Christina. 'We had good times there when you and Alexander were
young. You had your best growing years on Skorpios ... I don't want
ever to forget how it used be.'

Ari bought the island – 'a wild little rock,' he called it with affection
and pride – for $60,000 in 1963. 'We knew Skorpios,' Christina once
said, 'when the dust was thick on everything and everything was shrub.'
They had seen the villa being built, and watched the guest beach-houses
and stables going up. Each year when the *Christina* brought them back
for the summer idyll there was something new to surprise and excite
them. One year it was a whole farm with horses, goats, ducks and
rabbits. They had been the first to ride the mini-mokes on the new roads.
Christina had 'officially' opened the telephone exchange; Alexander
ceremoniously switched on the pumping station. 'My paradise,' Christina called Skorpios when she was sixteen. 'It's where I want to be when
I grow old.'

In an attempt to restore Christina's pre-Bolker eligibility, Ari had
particularly said he wanted 'a young bunch' on the island that summer
of '73. Florence Grinda, now estranged from the womanizing Jean-
Noël, came with her younger sister Caroline Michard-Pelissier, and
brother Hubert, who was studying to join his father's law firm; Marie
de Luynes, sister of the Duc de Chevreuse who had married Christine

Roussel, arrived with her sister-in-law's younger brother, Thierry.

Just turned twenty, Thierry Roussel – the eleven-year-old schoolkid Christina had first met at Florence Grinda's wedding – had grown into a lanky, full-of-himself fellow with thick blond hair, who was already showing signs that he had a way with women. (His present lover was a beautiful Swedish girl named Marianne 'Gaby' Landhage.) Christina displayed considerably more interest in Thierry now than she had nine years before. She pumped Florence to tell her everything she knew about him and his family.

The Roussels were a pharmaceutical manufacturing family belonging to that peculiarly French upper-middle-class aristocracy which is founded wholly on money. Thierry's father, Henri, had sold his share in the company (Roussel-Uclaf) to his elder brother, Jean-Claude, in order to consecrate the rest of his life to his favourite interest: shooting. He owned 10,000 acres just outside Marbella, a 700-acre sporting estate in the Sologne, France's best shooting country (President Valéry Giscard d'Estaing and Prince Bernhard of Lippe, father of Queen Beatrix of the Netherlands, were frequent guests) and a ranch in Kenya, as well as a house on the Indian Ocean coast. (All this and much of what follows Christina got from the well-informed Florence Grinda.) Thierry was educated at L'Ecole des Roches, one of the finest schools in France. He was best remembered for his prowess in the boxing ring – and for being a bit of a dandy (he was the first boy in the school to own a rabbit-fur coat). Brought up in Sologne and big-game Kenya, he had become, like his father, a first-class gun. He was also a keen falconer. But his boast that he had bagged the largest stag at Sologne lost some of its esteem when it was learned that he had bred the beast himself, waited until it was of prizewinning proportions, and then shot it. At twenty it was agreed that an interesting future awaited him.

'So Thierry came on the island,' Florence would later recall that summer on Skorpios. 'Christina always told me she wanted to marry a Frenchman, because she loved Paris, and because she wanted a blond, good-looking husband – she wanted to make a comparison with Caroline of Monaco.' Disturbed by Christina's romantic fixation on Roussel, who appeared to be perfectly cast for her dream, Florence strongly advised caution.

'I said to her, "Don't be crazy about him, he is with somebody else. He is not going to drop her, he is in love with that girl, and you are going to be very unhappy if you go on with this.' " It was so clear, the danger of that situation,' Florence Grinda remembered.

Little inclined to take any advice where men were concerned, Christina could not be persuaded that Thierry was not in all ways suitable. What was more, Ari totally approved of the young Frenchman and encouraged his daughter all the way. To help things along, he took Roussel into his study and showed him the plans for a new tanker, and broke down as he talked about the loss of his son. Ari could never resist an opportunity to test the irresistible power of his own will. And this broad hint that Thierry would find a ready place both in his family and in his business was not lost on Thierry, who quickly seduced the more than willing heiress who held the key to so much.

It must have been heady stuff for a young man who went to the island that summer with plenty of ambition but no clear idea where that ambition would lead him. When he invited Christina to visit him in Spain in September, she was sure she had landed him and that they would discuss only their future together. But Thierry, who had done a lot of thinking between Skorpios and Marbella, greeted her with the news that he was too much in love with Gaby to give her up even for such glittering prizes.

'At twenty,' said Ari philosophically when he was told of Roussel's unexpected turnabout, 'you make a lot of foolish mistakes.'

At twenty-three, Christina was not philosophical at all (except to admit that she had no gift for gauging lovers' feelings in these matters) and did not even try to hide her heartbreak. She turned for advice and solace to Philippe Niarchos.

Although their arranged love match had 'fallen at the first bedpost' (Christina's own private joke), her cousin was still a good and close friend and always there to comfort her when things went wrong. She liked his calm common sense; he also knew how to make her laugh. (Photographed together by an Italian paparazzo who demanded to know when they planned to marry, Philippe had answered dead-pan: 'As soon as possible. My future father-in-law is an agreeable old chap. To provoke a little good-natured anger in him, my father has said he will buy a whole Greek archipelago for us as a wedding present.')

It was nice, reliable, sensible Philippe who now turned her mind back to Peter Goulandris. Goulandris was Greek; he understood her in ways that other men never could, Philippe pointed out. And Goulandris knew the shipping business inside out.

This last point was not lost on Christina.

For some while now, since the death of Alexander, Ari's health had been in noticeable decline. (He had even decided to hold off on his plans for divorce until he felt stronger.) On the island that summer, he continued to drink his Black Label Scotch and sing the Greek ballads he loved to hear at night. But the old verve was not there. He complained of headaches all the time. When his guests had gone to bed, he would sit alone for hours on his haunches like a peasant beside Alexander's tomb. Christina knew that she was losing her father, and in more ways than one. She also knew that she was not ready to run the empire alone. That thought haunted her more than anyone guessed.

The tanker market had never been more exacting or more vulnerable as the Arabs continued to apply the greatest oil squeeze in history to discourage the West from aiding Israel in the fourth Arab–Israeli war. She knew how anxious her father had become. She had never known him to be so tense.

Perhaps he had hidden it better in the past, but now it showed in the strain that was in his face and in the bursts of anger with people who had known only his charm. More than a third of the Onassis tonnage was already laid up, and as country after country confronted the need to conserve fuel and began massive programmes to develop domestic resources and new energy technology, the depression would continue to deepen. She knew that none of the oil giants was interested in long-term charters; she knew that her father had just been forced to cancel an order for two ULCCs (ultralarge crude carriers) at a loss of $12.5 million. She knew he was having serious problems with Olympic Airways; and a refinery project in New Hampshire was going badly for him. And most of all she knew that there was no way she could begin to cope with these vast, diverse and complex problems on her own. (The fact that her father appeared to handle it all in his head with no more than a battered notebook to keep track of things unnerved her considerably.)

'Peter Goulandris?' Christina repeated thoughtfully, perhaps remembering the schoolgirl 'pash' she had on him, or the time she publicly stood him up for Danny Marentette. 'You really think he'd still be interested in me?' she asked.

'Of course he will,' Philippe Niarchos assured her.

She decided to move back to New York, where Peter Goulandris worked and lived with his mother. Ari was delighted with the news and immediately arranged for her to have a desk in his Manhattan office. He also gave her 'a very special gift' – her own personal maid, Eleni Syros. (Eleni had been with the Onassis family almost since Christina could remember; loaned to Maria Callas for a while, she returned to Avenue Foch shortly before Ari married Jackie in 1968.)

Ari had no doubts that a marriage would be arranged quickly. Any reservations Maria Goulandris might have (and after the engagement débâcle in 1970, it had to be assumed she would have some) would be overcome when he acquainted her with the sum of Christina's eventual inheritance: $1.2 billion, give or take.

The sad year of 1973 was coming to an end. It had been tough on everybody and they all wanted to put it behind them as soon as possible. Jackie, who was still, however fragilely, Mrs Aristotle Onassis, talked her husband into a trip to Acapulco. Christina avoided St Moritz, where her mother and Stavros were entertaining the four Niarchos children. Instead she went to Gstaad, where Mick Flick and his crowd, which included Gunther Sachs and his Swedish wife, Mirja, were staying. Now that she had made up her mind to marry Peter Goulandris, Christina felt more relaxed with Flick, and the mood between them that Christmas and New Year was the best it had ever been. Flick had no idea what had brought about the change in her (he no doubt suspected that it was not unconnected with the talk he had had with Johnny Meyer) and appeared to accept her story that she was going to live in the United States to pursue a career in journalism.

The atmosphere between Ari and Jackie in Acapulco was less relaxed, however. With his mind on the continuing crisis in the tanker trade, and his plans for a refinery in New Hampshire threatening to collapse at any moment, Ari had been in a foul mood throughout the whole holiday. And it had been rather foolish of Jackie to choose that time to tell her husband that she wanted to build a house in Acapulco – the place where she had spent her honeymoon with John F. Kennedy twenty years before. They were still arguing when they flew back to New York on 3 January. Ari eventually withdrew to a quiet corner of the private Learjet and beginning with the words, 'To my dear daughter,' started writing his last will and testament.

He bequeathed a lifetime income of $200,000 a year to Jackie (her children Caroline and John would each receive $25,000 a year until they were twenty-one) with the proviso that should she dispute the will or resort to the courts, she would immediately forfeit her annuity and his executors and the rest of his heirs were instructed to fight her 'through all possible legal means'. He outlined his plans for a foundation, in the name of his dead son, to promote welfare, religious, artistic and educational activities, for the most part in Greece, and to make annual awards based on the Swedish Nobel Prize system. The labyrinthine twist of corporations that he had manipulated and controlled all his life would ccasc to exist when he ceased to exist. His empire would continue in two new holdings to be called Alpha and Beta. Alpha would consolidate all his assets; Beta would contain only the shares in Alpha. Christina was to get all the assets in Alpha (plus an annual allowance of $250,000 and, on remarriagc, a further $50,000 a year for her husband). The controlling interest in Beta would go to the foundation, whose board of directors was to be drawn from his closest aides, headed by Costa Konialidis, and would, in effect, watch over the empire for Christina.

'My yacht, the *Christina*, if my daughter and wife so wish, they can keep for their personal use,' he concluded the long, comprehensive, carefully drafted document. If they found it too expensive to keep – and he estimated that it cost at least $600,000 a year to maintain – they were to present it to the Greek state. A similar clause covered the future of Skorpios. Jackie was to have a 25 per cent share in both the island and the yacht. As chief executor of the will he named: 'Athina, *née* Livanos, Onassis-Blandford-Niarchos, the mother of my son, Alexander.'

In February, Christina moved her base from Paris to New York, and began work in her father's office. She had never seen his operation at such close quarters before and the experience confirmed her worst nightmares about the interlocking intricacies of running an empire that included one of the world's biggest tanker fleets, an international airline company (the only national airline in the world owned by one man), a Fifth Avenue property corporation (Olympic Tower), and plans for a brand-new US refinery project. 'No wonder Daddy is getting headaches,' she said to Costa Gratsos, who had been put in charge of her business education.

But Christina was still inclined to blame Jackie for a good deal of her father's problems and misfortunes; she even warmed slightly towards

Maria Callas when the prima donna mischievously turned up in New York discussing her relationship with Ari, 'the greatest love of my life', with Barbara Walters on the *Today* television show. 'Love is so much better when you are not married,' she glinted meaningfully. Did she have any hard feelings about Jackie? 'Why should I? Of course, if she treats Mr Onassis very badly, I might be very angry,' Callas answered. Christina loved it.

In March, the New Hampshire state legislature finally turned down Ari's massive and ambitious refinery project. 'Well, that's one headache I don't have to worry about any more,' he put a brave face on his defeat for Christina. But like everyone else close to Ari at that time, she was appalled by his appearance. His head habitually slumped down against his chest, his eyes more hooded than usual, he looked constantly exhausted – 'as if he has just had all the life knocked out of his body,' Christina told Gratsos the day they got the bad news from New Hampshire. Even people who were used to his thick accent complained that he was mumbling and they couldn't understand what he was saying to them.

Christina persuaded him to get a check-up when the workload eased after the refinery project collapsed. For some while he had been living with a secret fear that he had muscular dystrophy. He was almost relieved when he learned that he had a disease he had never heard of before called myasthenia gravis, a disorder of the body's autoimmune system. Although incurable, it could be controlled by drugs. 'It usually hits men around their forties, so I take it as a tribute to my physical shape,' he said. In the beginning the new drugs seemed to work wonderfully as Ari regained a little of his old zest.

The summer in New York was a busy one also for Christina and Peter Goulandris, who had become 'an item' on the social circuit and the subjects of considerable speculation. Their rekindled friendship had become genuinely close. But Maria Goulandris was still a most powerful influence over her son and in spite of Ari's propaganda war she was not going to let him marry an Onassis without a fight. And this time Peter showed no willingness to defy his mother's wishes.

At work Gratsos was giving Christina high marks for effort. 'Already I trust her intuition more than my intelligence, probably even more than your sorcery,' he told Ari in June. It was certainly an exaggeration but the kindly Gratsos knew it was what Ari wanted to hear. But others in the organization were less enthusiastic and some were beginning to notice disturbing signs in her behaviour. 'One minute she'd be fine, smiling, relaxed – then wham! Her fuses were getting shorter all the time,' according to a colleague in the maritime insurance department of Frank B. Hall & Co, where she spent a month of her apprenticeship.

At the beginning of August, instead of taking off with Goulandris for Skorpios, where Ari was expecting them, she returned to London with Eleni. London in August is not at all the place to be for the kind of people Christina called her friends, and less than a handful of them knew where she was.

For twelve days she did not leave her house in Reeves Mews. A girlfriend in Paris who had been expecting an invitation to Skorpios thought she had disappeared with a lover. 'I hoped she was happy someplace,' she said.

But Christina was deeply and dangerously unhappy. For days she had refused to clean her teeth (an old childhood trick of rebellion and perhaps self-loathing) or even to get out of bed. And in the early hours of 16 August, Eleni called for an ambulance when she feared that Christina, who had not been making much sense for some while, was becoming comatose. At the Middlesex Hospital in London a massive overdose of sleeping pills was diagnosed, and her stomach pumped. She spent several hours in an intensive care unit before being transferred to a public ward under the name of C. Danai. Traced to the South of France, Tina returned to London in the Niarchos jet and, except for catnaps on a waiting room sofa, remained at her daughter's side for the next three days and nights. 'Why, why did you do this stupid thing?' she asked as soon as Christina was able to comprehend anything at all. 'Peter says he can never marry me,' Christina told her. 'I don't want to live.' Surprisingly, the drama was not discovered by the press; and not until she was out of danger and moved to a private room was even Ari informed.

Tina remained in London until Christina had completely recovered, then returned to the South of France. Her daughter's suicide bid, coming so soon after the suicide of Eugenie and the death of Alexander, took a great toll on her own meagre emotional reserves. She feared that a kind of retribution was at work. Her marriage to Niarchos had not been as happy as she had made it out to be to Ari. (She had only gone into it, she confided to her former lover Reinaldo Herrera, because Eugenie had spoken to her 'from beyond the grave' telling her to.) But she felt put

down by Niarchos's continuing flirtations with other women. Divorce
had been in her mind for several months.

On 21 September, at her husband's insistence, she returned to Paris
for a medical check-up. She was drinking heavily, and her increasing
dependency on drugs to put her to sleep and more drugs to wake her
up was a cause of growing concern in the family. Within months, it
seemed, her beauty had faded completely. 'Suddenly I'm forty-five years
old,' she told Christina plaintively the day she saw her doctors in Paris,
and finally confronted the actuality of middle age.

On the morning of Thursday, 10 October, Tina was found dead in
her bedroom in the Hôtel de Chanaleilles, the Niarchos Paris mansion.
Stavros Niarchos was asleep in another room. There were conflicting
reports about the cause of her death. In Paris, her secretary said the
cause of death was 'a heart attack, or a lung oedema' (excessive accumu-
lation of fluid in the tissues). A Niarchos spokesman in London
announced that she had 'a blood clot in one leg and that death resulted
when the clot moved to the heart obstructing blood circulation.' Christina was told the news in New York and flew to Paris immediately,
arriving in the early hours of Friday as newspapers were running stories
comparing her mother's death with the death of Eugenie on Spetsopoula
four years before.

The news agency Agence France Presse and the mass circulation
afternoon paper *France-Soir* had raised the possibility that death could
have been caused by an overdose of sleeping pills. The New York *Daily
News* ran a front-page story by its Paris correspondent Bernard Valéry,
who had known the family since the early days in Monaco, claiming
that 'sources close to Niarchos' admitted that her death was caused by
'an overdose of barbiturates and tranquillizers'. Most damaging of all
was one London report – totally false – that Stavros had been giving a
dinner party at the house while Tina lay dying in her bedroom.

Distressed and filled with anger and suspicion, Christina had by
11 a.m. obtained a magistrate's warrant ordering a postmortem examination. Ari, who had sown the seeds for his daughter's jaundiced view
of Niarchos, this time believed that his former brother-in-law was
guiltless. The two men issued a joint statement claiming that although
Christina had demanded the autopsy, the two families 'not only are not
opposed to it, but on the contrary welcome the decision.'

On 13 October two pathologists appointed by the public prosecutor's office confirmed without amplification that Tina had died from an acute oedema of the lung. The body, which showed no traces of violence, according to the London *Times*, was released for burial the same day. Ari did not attend the funeral at the Bois-de-Vaux cemetery in Lausanne, where Tina was laid to rest beside her sister. Niarchos wept throughout the service. Sunny, who had become the Duke of Marlborough five months after his divorce, was also in tears. It was to the Englishman that Christina turned when she broke down at the graveside. 'My aunt, my brother, now my mother – what is happening to us?' she sobbed.

Stavros Niarchos was not moved by Christina's grief. Still fuming at her intervention, on 14 October he had released a statement revealing for the first time details of her suicide attempt – 'at a time when her mother still mourned the death of her son. Tina never recovered from the depression into which these blows plunged her.' The significance of this public reproof was unmistakable: Christina herself had fatally aggravated her mother's already weakened condition.

Christina returned to New York. Peter Goulandris, still shaken by her suicide bid and feeling at least partly responsible, was back at her side. But too much had happened for their relationship ever to be the same again. And although they again talked of marriage, they realized that it was not only Maria Goulandris who stood in their way. It was a bad time for Christina, and in spite of Peter's optimistic talk of the future, she felt a sadness she could not shake; she frequently burst into tears in the middle of dinner or while walking along the street.

One reason for her depression was that her father's health had gone into a rapid decline after Tina's death. The drugs were no longer able to control the symptoms of his illness. He returned to hospital in New York using the name Mr Phillips. When his eyelids became too weak to stay open, Christina cut strips of Band-Aid to tape them up and, aware of his vanity, ordered even darker lenses for his glasses to hide the plaster. 'This is God punishing you for all your sins,' she teased him. 'I never think about sin,' he told her, his voice gruff with age and nicotine. 'It's my nature,' he said.

Although his executives continued to issue optimistic bulletins about his health, and played down the seriousness of his disease, the thought of death was often close to Ari's mind. A few weeks before his hospitalization in November he had taken Hélène Gaillet to his son's tomb on Skorpios. 'It wasn't a sad visit,' the New York socialite and photographer later recalled. 'He talked as if he expected him to join us any minute. "Alexander is just as living to me as you are. He comes to me often. Unfortunately, till I die I cannot go to him," he said.' He had, for a brief moment, she added, 'a haunted face, a look of terrible longing'.

Although his face was badly swollen from cortisone injections prescribed to counter decreased adrenal function, he insisted on discharging himself from the hospital after only five days. 'One ailing Aristotle Onassis is equal to six good men,' he told Costa Gratsos, who had been summoned to the hospital by Christina to try to talk her father out of going home in his present condition. But behind the braggadocio, Ari was a frightened man, frightened for himself, for his daughter and for his empire. On top of everything else, the increase in oil prices had hit his Olympic airline harder than most other carriers, since the threat of war with Turkey over Cyprus that summer had very nearly destroyed the vital Greek tourist trade. Even so, he had taken little interest in the company since Alexander's death, and had no idea how critical the situation had become. The day on which he discharged himself from the hospital, Olympic began cutting many of its regular schedules for want of cash. It was the first time he realized how much trouble his airline was in. His rage was awesome, and his rages were notorious at the Olympic headquarters on Fifth Avenue (his habit of pushing the ground-floor button and arriving in the basement and not at street level as in Europe had caused such tantrums that the Olympic elevators had to be rewired European-style). The Olympic crisis followed the less than triumphant opening of Olympic Tower, a fifty-two-storey Fifth Avenue condominium, which he had built in association with the Arlen Realty Corporation. He knew that the midtown skyscraper was always going to be a risk at a time of inflation and deepening recession. But less than forty of the 230 apartments had been sold, and the apartments unashamedly designed for the very rich were having to be hyped 'with a promotion campaign rarely equalled even in the real estate industry,' according to the *Wall Street Journal*.

As a daughter, and as an executive, Christina had reached a closeness with her father she hadn't known before. Throughout that year she had accompanied him to meetings and business dinners in New York, London and Paris. ('My father told me I had to listen to every word, to observe, and to keep my mouth closed until I knew what I was talking

Christina, who entered the world against all the odds, wanted by neither her mother nor her father, is baptized in New York, aged eleven months.

Happy families: Alexander and Christina flank grandfather Stavros Livanos. Cousin Philippe Niarchos, Christina's once and future lover, is in the foreground.

A family that flies together does not necessarily stay together: the Onassises land in Nice, 1955.

Christina, aged
seven, and her
mother pose aboard
the yacht *Christina*:
'Tina was ashamed
of having produced
such a daughter,'
remembers a friend.

Out of sight, but
Maria Callas was
never out of Ari's
mind.

It was unlikely that Tina would have had to reach for her *Debrett's* to have at least a passing knowledge of the Marquess of Blandford.

Ari and his *Chryso mou* ('My golden one') and his son, Alexander. It was no secret that they blamed Maria Callas for breaking up their parents' marriage.

'It's a perfect match,'
Alexander tells his little
sister at their father's
wedding on Skorpios in 1968.
'Our father loves names and
Jackie loves money.'

Baroness Thyssen-Bornemisza was
Alexander's mistress and Christina's mentor.

Face the music and
dance: Christina and
Ari.

First love: Danny
Marentette.

Luis Sosa Basualdo took her home in a taxi and didn't even kiss her goodnight.

Luis Sosa Basualdo ('Gaucho' to his friends) was gratified at the susceptibility he had touched off in Christina.

Lunch date: Basualdo and Christina at the Corviglia Club, 1971.

Just turned twenty, Thierry Roussel was already showing signs that he had a way with women – and especially with Christina.

Mick Flick preferred blondes: his earnest disinclination to go to bed with Christina became an open secret.

Les copains: with pal Florence Grinda at a Monaco soirée.

Peter Goulandris: the pre-honeymoon went well but Christina got tired of everyone trying to marry her off.

It wasn't, Joseph Bolker admitted, the most eager proposal of marriage he had ever made in his life.

Christina's melancholy deepened into despair as she watched her father fading.

Nowhere to hide: Christina and Jackie are caught by photographers as they leave the American Hospital in Paris where Ari lay dying.

With cousin Philippe Niarchos ... lovers no more.

With Alexander Andreadis, husband number two: 'My heart skipped a beat the moment he said hello,' Christina confessed.

Unsuited ... Andreadis was a great disappointment to her.

Nobody saw Sergei Kauzov coming.

Sergei and Christina announce their engagement in Moscow.

Sergei would soon discover how wayward Christina's love could be.

Skorpios: The gang's all here: the Kauzovs, Alberto Dodero (*standing back right*), Marina Dodero (*with flower in her hair*), Yuri the dog, Claude Roland.

ABOVE LEFT Christina had a $1000-a-day Diet Coke habit.

ABOVE RIGHT With lawyer Hubert Michard-Pelissier: 'Lovers, no. Best friends, yes.'

RIGHT Christina loved to dance.

Claude Roland and the girl who came to supper.

Perfume heir Yvon Coty scented romance.

Nicky Mavroleon: their affair became the talk of St Moritz.

TOP Luis Luis and little Clare: they danced all night when Christina called the tune.

BELOW The hole in the wall gang: Alberto and Marina Dodero, daughter Carmen, Clare Lawman, Christina, Luis Basualdo.

ABOVE Thierry Roussel: 'I've waited ten years for this man,' Christina said.

RIGHT 'We are wonderfully in love,' Christina said, hugging husband number four.

LEFT Christina had a fine business mind when she put her mind to a deal.

Gaby Landhage: mother of Erik and Sandrine Roussel.

RIGHT Happy bikers: James Blandford, Daphne Guinness, Luis Basualdo.

BELOW Christophe Gollut and the beautiful Andrea de Montal face the camera with Christina.

Mother and child.

ABOVE Model Ula joins up with
Thierry and Christina on the isle
of Capri.

RIGHT Christina's last date,
Jorge Tchomlekdjoglou: he
positively bloomed – she
wanted the rumours to irritate
Roussel.

The last formal picture: taken in Buenos Aires on 16 November 1988, at a fund-raising gala at the residence of the Uruguayan ambassador to Argentina.

about,' she later explained her routine silence to BP chairman Sir Eric Drake.) Now for the first time in her life she had first-hand knowledge of the stress her father was under as he wheeled and dealed, charmed and bullied his way through the corporate jungles.

And certainly she had picked up enough to know exactly what was at stake when Constantine Karamanlis, whose New Democracy party had just swept to power in Athens in the first free elections since 1964, turned down Ari's request for a massive injection of government money into Olympic Airways. Ari responded by grounding the entire Olympic fleet, freezing salaries, and threatening to wash his hands of the whole business. It was a familiar ploy, only this time it did not work. The prime minister, who believed that Ari's relationship with the deposed colonels far exceeded the ordinary requirements of business tact, appointed an emergency management board and announced that the government would open immediate negotiations to repossess the national airline.

Christina knew that the loss of Olympic was a failure appalling to contemplate and impossible to ignore. Even so she did her best to dissuade her father from returning to Athens in December in his final bid to keep control of the airline that he had so often claimed he did not want. She was hurt when he refused to let her accompany him. 'Those bastards will think you're there because I need a nurse,' he told her with more unkindness than perhaps he intended. Later Christina came up with an interesting theory why her father did not want her, or Jackie, to accompany him to Athens. 'By December, he knew he was going to lose the airline,' she said. 'After twenty years, it was going to be taken away from him. He was going to fight because he always fought, but he knew he couldn't win. He didn't want us to see him beaten.'

On 15 January 1975, while Jackie was skiing with her son John on the Swiss slopes of Crans-sur-Sierre, and Christina was shopping in Gstaad with Peter Goulandris and his mother, Ari formally handed back Olympic Airways to the Greek government.

Five days later, on 20 January, probably but not positively his seventy-fifth birthday, Ari recognized that time was running out for him. On that day he spoke to his daughter in Gstaad and set in motion the grand design that would secure his empire for ever. On the understanding that he would divorce Jackie, he extracted a promise from Christina that she would marry Peter Goulandris, to whom she had been unofficially and nearly engaged on a number of occasions. 'Think about it, Johnny, the greatest tanker fleet the world has seen,' he crowed to Meyer as once again he attempted to achieve his dream of a G&O alliance. But the strain of those weeks in which he fought to keep control of his airline caught up with him sooner than he expected. On 3 February he collapsed in Athens with severe abdominal pains.

Christina returned to Athens immediately; Jackie flew back from New York. It was at once apparent that Ari was very sick indeed. His body weight had dropped forty pounds in eight weeks. His speech was slurred; he needed to hold his chin to help him talk at all. The immediate cause of his collapse was an attack of gallstones. But because of his poor condition, caused partly by the myasthenia gravis which made it difficult for him to chew, partly by his neglecting to eat regularly during the takeover battle, and a bout of flu, he was in an 'extremely vulnerable' state. Moreover, specialists summoned from Paris and New York could not agree among themselves about the best way to go. The French liver specialist Professor Jean Caroli wanted to operate at once to remove Ari's gall bladder; heart specialist Dr Isidore Rosenfeld believed he was too feeble to undergo major surgery.

Ari himself made the decision to return to Paris and have his gall bladder removed at the American Hospital in Neuilly. On the afternoon of 6 February, accompanied by Christina and Jackie, he left the Glyfada villa for the airport clutching a book called *Supership*, in which author Noel Mostert reported that the first million-ton tanker, a ship so big that a cathedral could be lost in its bowels, would soon become a reality. Ari sat with the book unopened on his lap for most of the flight; memories of the *Ariston*, the 15,000-ton 'monster' they said was impossible when he built her in the 1930s, must have been in his mind.

The familiar paparazzi waiting outside 88 Avenue Foch were joined this dry, almost balmy February evening by five television crews, photographers from *Paris-Match*, *Stern*, *Oggi* and many other international magazines and newspapers as well as the simply curious. It was very plain. Aristotle Socrates Onassis had returned to Paris for the last time. 'I want to walk from this car under my own steam,' Ari said to his wife and daughter when he saw the press watch. 'I don't want those sons of bitches to see me being held up by a couple of women.'

Christina's melancholy deepened into despair as she watched him climb the steps, and, unaided, go inside. The supreme effort, his last big show for the press, took everything he had. He went straight to bed, and slept for several hours. When he awoke, shortly after 10 p.m., he took a Pyridostigmine slow-release capsule to get him through the night; the capsule released one-third (sixty milligrams) of its dosage immediately and gave him a surge of energy into which he crammed as much business as he could manage, and saw the people he wanted to see. One of the people he sent for on this night was Johnny Meyer. They talked about the past, swapped familiar anecdotes. After one long silence when Meyer thought he had fallen asleep, Ari said: 'Soon I shall be on Skorpios with Alexander.' 'You're crazy, Ari,' Meyer replied. 'Who ever heard of anybody dying from droopy eyelids.' Christina was waiting in the hall for Meyer when he left Ari's room close to tears. She asked him to arrange a suite for her at the Hôtel Plaza-Athenée. She did not want to share the apartment with Jackie, she said, after her father had checked into the American Hospital.

Shortly before midday Ari left in a blue Peugeot from the underground garage and began the short journey to the hospital on Boulevard Victor Hugo. As the photographers and reporters at the main gate were distracted by the arrival of Christina and Jackie, he entered the hospital unobserved through the adjacent chapel, known to interns as the 'artists' exit', since it is also the route to the morgue.

His gall bladder was removed on Sunday, 9 February. Christina, who had moved into the Plaza-Athenée, also took a room next to her father's first-floor suite in the hospital's Eisenhower wing. She spent most of her time by his bedside with her favourite aunt, Ari's closest sister, Artemis. Clannish and exacting, the two Greek women made Jackie feel like an intruder in the presence of her husband. Jackie, as she always did to ease her nerves, affected insouciance, and not for the first time was misunderstood by Christina and her aunts.

At the end of the month, a hospital bulletin revealed 'a slow but progressive improvement' in Ari's condition. Reassured, Jackie returned to New York to see her daughter. She telephoned every day to check his progress and was told that his condition remained serious but stable.

On the morning of 10 March, Ari was alert enough to call his daughter *Chryso mou* – it was the last time she would hear those words on his lips – and, although he could barely speak, to remind her of her promise to marry Peter Goulandris.

That evening Christina and Peter Goulandris went through the traditional Greek 'giving word of marriage' ceremony and afterwards went to Ari's bedside to give him the news and receive his blessing.

Five days later Aristotle Socrates Onassis was dead.

———

Jackie hurried back from New York, accompanied by her mother, her children, and Teddy Kennedy. At Orly she issued a fifty-three-word statement: 'Aristotle Onassis rescued me at a moment when my life was engulfed with shadows. He meant a lot to me. He brought me into a world where one could find both happiness and love. We lived through many beautiful experiences together which cannot be forgotten, and for which I will be eternally grateful.'

'How long did she spend with my father?' Christina wanted to know when she was told that Jackie had been to the hospital chapel where Ari was lying in state, with a Greek Orthodox icon on his chest. Informed that Jackie had made the sign of the cross and prayed by Ari's body for seven minutes, she said: 'is that all – sixty seconds for every year of their marriage? Couldn't she spare him even ten minutes at the end?'

Jackie's ability always to hide her feelings was the antithesis of Christina's own volatile Levantine nature. (Her left wrist was heavily bandaged when she left the hospital the day her father died, and it was rumoured that in an agony of grief she had again tried to kill herself.) That Jackie had been 3,000 miles away when Ari died Christina took as a measure of the distance that had come between her father and stepmother. (She totally ignored the fact that she and aunt Artemis had deliberately been misleading Jackie in New York about Ari's deteriorating condition, even after 10 March, when they were advised that he was not expected to live more than a matter of days.)

A Boeing 727 carried Ari's body home to Greece. And in spite of the evident chill between them during the recent days in Paris, Christina shared a limousine with Jackie and Teddy Kennedy in the cortège of cars and buses on the journey to the fishing village of Nidri where Ari's body was to be placed on a launch for the last ride to Skorpios. Women in black shawls lined the route, church bells tolled. Suddenly the motorcade came to a halt. Christina left the limousine she was sharing with her stepmother and got into the car behind. In a little while, the cortège of cars continued on its way. It was more than a decade before the reason for that extraordinary episode on the journey to Nidri was revealed. According to one of Christina's closest friends in Paris, Teddy Kennedy had attempted to raise the question of Jackie's inheritance. 'Christina knew that Teddy wasn't there to share her grief, to hold Jackie's hand. He was there for a specific purpose; he was going to want to discuss business sooner or later. Ari always had money in his head, Christina understood that ... the Kennedys had it in their hearts, she understood that, too. But Teddy's timing blew her mind. And that's why she hightailed it out of the limo that day.'

The service on Skorpios was a simple one. Christina had asked the village priest to read St Paul's Epistle to the Thessalonians ... 'I went to the grave and I saw the naked bones, and I said to myself, who are you? King or soldier? Rich or poor? Sinner or just?' Employees in their work clothes – chefs and waiters, gardeners and sailors and maids – stood side by side with the rich and famous as the body of Aristotle Socrates Onassis was lowered into a concrete vault alongside his son Alexander's.

As the sun went down and the breeze began to blow off the Aegean, the heiress stood on the deck of the *Christina* and told the crew and all the employees gathered around her: 'This boat and this island are mine. You are all my people now.'

—9—

*I am all the daughters of my father's
house
And all the brothers too*

William Shakespeare
Twelfth Night

PEOPLE WHO UNDERESTIMATED CHRISTINA ONASSIS on the basis of her rich girl's bent for triviality, or the folly of her marriage to Joseph Bolker, or even her gender, soon changed their minds when they saw the way she poured herself into the business of unravelling her legacy. The day after her father was buried on Skorpios, she flew to Switzerland to stay with Peter Goulandris at the estate outside Lausanne of his uncle, Basil Goulandris. A spokesman in Monte Carlo described the visit as 'a few days' rest' after the harrowing weeks she had spent watching her father die in Paris. But through the death of her family she was not only embarking on a voyage of self-discovery and what it meant to be an Onassis but also releasing energies within herself that were changing her whole personality. Johnny Meyer recalled the precise moment when he recognized her transformation: 'She called at three o'clock in the morning to ask me to do something for her. Only Ari would have had the crust to do that. I told myself, "This kid's really got what it takes." She was making up for lost time, and loving every minute.'

Rest was the last thing Christina had in mind in Lausanne.

On her marriage to Stavros Niarchos, her mother had entrusted to him her personal fortune (reputed to be worth $75 million); after Tina's death he claimed that she had 'given' the money to him. After consulting her lawyers in Geneva, Christina launched a lawsuit in Athens to have her mother's marriage annulled on the grounds that it was unlawful for her to have wed her brother-in-law. She also claimed that the marriage was not valid since Tina had been Niarchos's fourth wife, and that is a bride too far in Greek law. But money was not completely the reason

90

for Christina's attack. She was also getting even for the way Niarchos had disclosed her suicide bid in London to the whole world.

Satisfied with the start she had made, Christina took off with Goulandris to spend Easter on the Bahaman island of Eleuthers, where Peter had rented a villa at the Windermere Island Club. The pre-honeymoon went well: they swam, played tennis, made love, and endlessly discussed their future together. Goulandris too saw the extraordinary change in her since Ari's death. Her confidence was remarkable. 'I want to be my own woman,' she said. 'I'm not responsible to anyone other than myself,' she repeated, like a mantra. At the bar one evening she overheard two salvage experts complaining about Greek shipping standards after a Greek-registered tanker had run aground on a local island causing a great deal of pollution. Before Goulandris could stop her, she went across to the men and berated them for their remarks. One of the experts snapped back, 'Who do you think you are, Onassis?' A triumphant grin spread across Christina's face. 'That's *exactly* who I am,' she said, and went back to her table.

Only the Goulandris family continued to be unimpressed with the new-style Christina. She would always be the daughter of Ari, the perpetual outsider, the man they mockingly called 'the parachutist' because he fell among them out of nowhere. They refused to accept the validity of the engagement, made, they felt, under the emotional blackmail of Ari's deathbed. Arch-conservatives, they could not forgive Christina for being a divorcee. Nevertheless, only a period of mourning had prevented the marriage from already having taken place. But by the middle of April, getting from his own family the sort of pressure that Ari had once put on Joseph Bolker, Peter Goulandris's doubts had returned.

But Christina too was having a change of heart, and it was she who finally announced the end of the engagement. 'I am tired of everyone trying to marry me off. It isn't because it's too soon after my father's death but because I don't have plans to marry Peter [Goulandris] or anyone else,' she declared. That powerful business considerations had been at work there is no doubt (it was clear that the tanker recession was not going to go away for a very long time and a Goulandris–Onassis alliance would have been, in the words of one Athens shipping broker, 'the biggest merger of white elephants in the world'), but they were not entirely responsible for Christina's decision.

Christina had no time for tears, or emotional postmortems. On 29 April, at the American Embassy in Paris, she renounced her United States citizenship, which had exposed her world-wide income to American taxes under a law dating back to 1962 and the Kennedy administration. But in abandoning her American birthright and the long arm of the Internal Revenue Service, she created another problem for herself. She was the sole beneficiary of the trust that controlled Victory Carriers, the American company set up as part of the settlement of a criminal litigation instituted against Ari by the Justice Department in the 1950s. And that agreement specifically excluded foreign participation in profits from the company's four American-flagged tankers. Her solution was a piece of pure legerdemain of which Ari himself would have been proud. The ships, operating in the volatile spot market, would continue to be controlled by Costa Gratsos in New York; a second trust would be created to hold Victory Carriers, and the beneficiaries of that trust would be the American Hospital in Paris. 'It looks to us like a tax dodge for Christina,' admitted hospital director Perry Cully. Ten years afterwards, the first dollar had still to find its way from the trust to the hospital coffers.

This was characteristic of the speed and decisiveness of her decisions. Even the ageing cadre of cousins and old cronies who ostensibly ruled the Onassis empire was impressed. 'She is going to be one of the most expert shipping people in the world in a very few years, capable of running all of these things without the advice of old, dilapidated men,' Costa Gratsos told *The New York Times* on 15 June. It was the line he had fed to Ari – only now he 'seemed to have a little more faith in what he was saying,' according to an Olympic staffer in New York.

'You should have told them that my father left me plenty of problems to practise on,' she kidded Gratsos the day she read his interview in the *Times*. Among those problems was the state of Olympic's tanker fleet. Thirteen of its fifteen supertankers were on long-term charters to oil majors, and chalking up huge profits despite the tanker glut. But seven of those charters were due to run out in the next two years. In New York she appointed Eliot Bailen, who had been Ari's counsellor since the 1950s, and was now with the law firm Holtzmann, Wise and Shepherd, to set up a special 'task force' to review the situation and prepare a 'crisis plan' for the next five years.

She also began a diligent study of the way her empire was run. It was a most tangled web. Olympic Maritime, for example, which ran the day-to-day shipping side of the business out of a *belle époque* building in Monte Carlo, with a staff of 150, was merely a branch of a dummy corporation registered in Panama. Another sixty-five people worked for the Springfield Shipping Company in Athens. They were responsible for hiring crews and provisioning the fleet, and operated out of a tenement building in the port of Piraeus. Each of the ships was run as a separate corporation, usually registered in Panama to avoid taxes. There was no central accounting system; the ledgers for one corporation were usually kept in the offices of another a continent away; profits were moved through a labyrinth of tax-haven shells.

Grappling with all this information (and there can be no doubt that even after months of apprenticeship at her father's side, much of it was new and eye-opening to her), Christina still had time to deal with the outstanding problems of inheritance with her stepmother. She came straight to the point in a fifteen-minute meeting with Jackie in New York: how much did Jackie want for her share in the yacht and the island, and to renounce all further claims to the Onassis estate? Jackie was ready to do business, and a ballpark figure was quickly agreed. ('They were two sharp ladies who recognized that a settlement was not only possible but palpably pragmatic,' said an Onassis banker in New York.) Jackie returned to Skorpios to collect her personal things, her mementos of Ari, and to close down the pink house he had built for her seven years before. It would take eighteen months of legal toing and froing to settle the final figure of $26 million, and Meyer said when it was over: 'It was a steep price to pay, but Christina didn't complain. She wanted to expunge the very thought of Jackie.' Yet Christina, who would always be deeply ambivalent about her stepmother, always kept in touch, even attending John's confirmation service.

Christina's willpower and fresh vigour surprised everybody. Never had she been more bursting with energy or more euphoric. She appeared to deal with the complexities of her inheritance and the difficulties in her private affairs with an aplomb and a sureness that seemed out of the question to those who knew that her emotional stability had for a long time been threatened. But there was an ominous hint that she was storing up trouble for herself in her increasing use of medication. It began in the trying days after her father's death when, following the incident at the hospital in which she cut her own wrist, her uncle, Dr

Theodore Garofalides, prescribed the antidepressant drug Imipramine. But the side effects left her weary and depleted; and to overcome her exhaustion she turned to amphetamines, and later she began using barbiturates to sleep. Eventually, the pills lost their potency, and in an attempt to break the vicious circle of more and more uppers and downers, she began taking shots. Unable to face the ordeal of sticking a needle into herself, a private nurse was put on the payroll, to travel with her everywhere to administer the injections. 'She was forever trying to wake up or go to sleep,' complained a Paris lover. Also complaining were Olympic staffers who were again becoming victims of her sudden mood swings as she repeated the behavioural pattern that preceded her flight to London the previous August. In fact, she would admit later, she felt 'very near to suicide'.

She met her saviour in the coffee shop at the Athens Hilton Hotel. The hotel was owned by the Andreadis family, headed by seventy-year-old Professor Stratis Andreadis, a well-known Athenean reputed to have a $600 million fortune from shipping, the Commercial Bank of Greece, the country's largest private bank, and minerals. The professor also had three sons, the youngest of whom was named Alexander, and he was checking out the action at the hotel when he saw Christina. They hadn't met for a decade and she offered to buy him a coffee. Of average height, overweight by around 30 pounds and with Presley-style sideburns framing his pink pudgy cheeks, Alexander had a remarkable impact on Christina. 'My heart skipped a beat the moment he said hello,' she later remembered.

It was true that the lovers must have at once recognized many things in each other. Their fathers had both enjoyed close relations with the military junta. It was Stratis Andreadis who inherited the refinery contract after Ari lost it – only to lose it himself when Papadopoulos was kicked out in 1973. The colonel's successor also repealed Alexander's military service deferment, and at the age of thirty he still had nearly a year to do in the ranks when he met Christina.

Eight days after the meeting at the Hilton they announced their engagement. 'I think I asked Alexander to marry me when I told him I couldn't live without him,' Christina later recalled. 'He said, "Then why don't we get married?" I was thunderstruck.'

The announcement came at an opportune time for Stratis Andreadis. Behind his appearance of laconic affluence and reliability the professor was a nervous man. Following the collapse of the junta, and the disappearance of many of his powerful friends, his business affairs were being scrutinized by officials from the Bank of Greece. Serious charges of fraud seemed inevitable. The Onassis millions would certainly help to give an injection of tangibility and hope to his name when the crisis was revealed.

So far none of this was known outside a small circle of banking and government officials. (In London, the *Financial Times* pondered: 'Although this is not one of those carefully arranged Greek dynastic marriages, and the pair only met apparently a month ago, it looks as if there is new management and financial muscle behind the Onassis interests.') But there is little doubt that the Onassis uncles suspected the worst. Yet their disapproval served merely to give the romance an added piquancy in Christina's eyes.

At sunset on 22 July, the lovers were married in the private Byzantine chapel of the summer residence of Prince Peter of Greece at Glyfada. Jackie was among the guests: 'I do love that child. I'm so happy Christina has found Alexander. At last I see happy days ahead for her,' she is supposed to have gushed. But Jackie's presence, with her son, John, merely indicated the lengths they were prepared to go to convey unity and confidence instead of anxiety and division within the family. Ari had been dead three months, the family was still in mourning. And as Christina, in a primrose yellow dress, and pinstripe-suited Alexander made the traditional three trips around the altar and were pronounced man and wife, it was the memory of a death that hung like a shadow over the tiny congregation. 'You can't excuse Christina, but it's hard not to pity her,' somebody said.

Alexander claimed that there was no time for a honeymoon – his bride had planned to take the *Christina* to the Caribbean – as he had to report back to his army unit on the Greco-Turkish border. The real reason was not so patriotic. He was facing trial, along with his father and eight others, including former junta chief George Papadopoulos (who was also on trial in another court for treason), on serious charges of violating and destroying property. The action had been brought by farmers who accused the Andreadises of using their close links with the former dictators to steal their land. Hours before the wedding the farmers were granted an order forbidding Alexander to leave the country.

Such was the rush to the altar that Christina received the wedding band before her husband could find an engagement ring that would reflect his aspirations (and before he could inform his regular girlfriend, Denise Sioris, who lived in Washington). Calls to jewellers in Paris and Athens produced a 19-carat diamond, said to have come from the collection of the late King Farouk of Egypt, valued at $750,000. But expensive baubles, like precipitant passion, are no guarantee of domestic harmony. It was not long before their private problems became public knowledge.

In September, noonday shoppers in Paris were treated to a kerbside squabble as Alexander attempted to stop Christina entering a boutique, insisting that she join him and some friends for lunch at Maxim's around the corner. 'For the last time, I don't feel like eating,' she yelled at him for all the Champs Elysées to hear. He grabbed her by the arm and bundled her into a waiting limousine. At Maxim's, pretending to go to the ladies' room, she left the restaurant, did her shopping, and returned ninety minutes later to her furious husband. And six weeks after that there was a spectacular row in the lobby of Monte Carlo's Hôtel de Paris where Christina insisted on playing backgammon with friends until 4 a.m. Finally Alexander hurled the board across the lobby, and dragged his erring wife to the elevator. Nor can the couple's fragile harmony have been helped when her uncles persuaded Christina to publicly distance the Onassis empire from the Andreadis banks and businesses. At a press conference called ostensibly to confirm her personal control of the Onassis empire, she made it crystal clear that her fortune would not be merged with the Andreadis assets or interests in any way.

In November it was reported that Christina was pregnant. The baby was due in May – a son, she told friends, who would be named after her father. But within weeks she was angrily denying the story, even to those whom she herself had confided the news. French newspapers speculated that she had suffered a miscarriage; but close friends of the Andreadises were convinced that, deeply worried about the fallibility of the marriage, she had had another abortion.

Less than six months had gone by since her 'heart skipped a beat' when Alexander said hello, yet she was already preparing to kiss him goodbye. Her second marriage had been as great a disappointment to her as her first. What made this one far worse was that the Andreadis scandal was now out in the open, and more serious than she had been led to believe when Alexander forewarned her of a delicate situation in the family. Three of the Andreadis banks had been placed under government control; Stratis Andreadis, already exposed as a cheat who had hired others to write the theses and articles which secured his professorship, was being investigated by the public prosecutor for alleged embezzlement and violation of currency rules.

The Andreadis crisis (at Olympic Maritime it was referred to as the Andreadis Fault) temporarily saved the marriage, since Christina was reluctant to leave Alexander at such a pressured time. They spent Christmas together in St Moritz. Christina rented the Villa Vittodorum in Suvretta, near the Villa Marguns of Stavros Niarchos, whom she was still pursuing through the courts for her mother's missing millions. If Alexander had hopes of reaching a better understanding with his wife in new romantic surroundings in the season of goodwill he was to be disappointed. An accomplished and enthusiastic skier, Christina found that Alexander was as ungainly and unattractive to her on the slopes as she had found him to be in the ordinary walks of life. (Since paying 7,000 drachmas to buy himself out of the army under a new government ruling Alexander had grown fat.) Leaving him in the hands of an instructor, Christina skied the high mountains with uncle George and Willy, his guide, who knew every run for twenty miles. St Moritz is not a town for secrets, and very soon the seriousness of the split between Christina and Alexander was common gossip. 'I have seen them have violent arguments and upsets which could be construed by people as being more serious than in fact they are,' insisted Nigel Neilson, who had been a mouthpiece for Ari, and was now employed by Christina. 'By their very nature, Christina and Alexander are extremely strong characters and they stand up to each other over everything. But this has not shaken their bond to each other,' he said, confirming that Christina would continue to stick by her husband – at least in his hour of need.

But Alexander sealed his own fate that summer. A motorbike enthusiast, he fractured his right leg when he crashed on Skorpios. It was a serious injury; there were fears for his limb. He was flown from Actium to Athens in the new $2 million Learjet Christina had acquired in America at Easter. Thigh-high in plaster for three months, a sexual relationship was out of the question. Christina whiled away the time with Peter Goulandris, who had reappeared in her life after an absence of fifteen months. Although the dalliance did not rekindle ideas of marriage to her old flame, it stiffened her resolve to get rid of Alexander. At the end of September, after thirteen months of marriage, she told her husband that she was filing for divorce.

While Alexander continued to grow fat and waited miserably in Athens, brooding over the scandal that threatened the family fortune, Christina was convinced that everything was going her way again. Photographed with Mick Flick in Paris, she was asked whether love was better the second time around. 'I've decided to marry eight times,' she answered deadpan. 'There is plenty of time to find out.' She flew to Japan with Costa Gratsos (the man who had sold Ari's whaling fleet in the 1950s for $15 million when all Ari expected was $3.5 million) to renegotiate contracts for tankers which her father had ordered in the boom years but which were now an embarrassment. Gratsos got a settlement that delighted Christina. She celebrated with Imelda Marcos at the Malacañang Palace in Manila.

Signs that the negotiations with Niarchos were also reaching a satisfactory conclusion came when Christina returned to Paris and gave a party for sixty guests at Maxim's – including Stavros, albeit placed further down the table than was his custom. The guest list reflected the intensity and glamour of her social life. She placed herself between Baron Guy de Rothschild, doyen of the banking dynasty, and Count Freddie Chandon, the champagne tsar. Another guest gave a glimpse of her lifestyle as well as her impulsive personality: 'We are platonic friends,' said Claude Roland. 'She invites herself to dinner with me at my apartment and brings her own food, maybe oysters and a salad, and butler, as well as some wine and Coca-Cola, in case I don't have any.'

That Christmas, Christina returned to St Moritz alone and feeling pretty damn pleased with herself. She moved into her new home, Villa Cristal, which her friend Atalanta Politis had just finished decorating. She made an effort to cut down on the stuff her nurse was continuing to shoot into her. 'I feel free maybe for the first time ever,' she said. 'I've got my friends around me and I'm on track. I'm not going to mess up again.' Another good reason for her optimism was the fact that Niarchos had agreed to return her mother's inheritance, although it had been left to him legally in her will. ('"Do what you want, take all the money," my father eventually told Christina,' Constantine Niarchos remembered later. 'He said, "I don't want any of it."')

If Christmas 1976 was especially low-key, the parties fewer, it was because Christina was 'gathering my strength for the ides of March.' Her divorce case was set for March, and she knew that her prepared statement would make unpleasant headlines when it was read out in the Athens court by her lawyer. And she was right. Accusing her husband of being a motorbike freak was a mild preamble to a harangue that included the view that he was 'despotic, foul-mouthed, blindly jealous and yet a womanizer, and fanatically self-centred'. Andreadis replied in kind. Christina had 'a peculiar and dictatorial character and really didn't care about me,' he claimed. 'She often called me a peasant and I was fed up with her talking about her boats all the time.'

The divorce was granted in July on the ground of mutual incompatibility.

'I'm through with marriage and romance,' she said. 'I won't let anything stand in the way of running my business now. That is the one major goal in my life. I have no intention of letting down the family name. The business will grow in size and profits.' At first she appeared to be as good as her word. Part of the $50 million insurance money she collected on the *Olympic Bravery*, which ran aground on her maiden voyage (and fortuitously avoided running up losses of almost $10 million a year in the depressed tanker market), she used to buy a 270,000-ton tanker from Daniel K. Ludwig. It was her first splash on the tanker scene in her own right. But it seemed an extraordinary and risky buy (especially from a man, one of the five richest people in the world, known to be among the shrewdest operators in the business). It was difficult to see how she could emerge a winner from the deal, even though she got the ship for $10 million less than its current value, and more than $50 million less than it would have cost in the peak years. 'In shipping,' she later quoted one of her father's maxims, 'the advantage is always to the one with the most patience.' She calculated that even if she had to lay up the new tanker (renamed *Aristotle Onassis*) for five years, she would still make a quick killing with it when the market recovered.

An indication of the determined state of Christina's mind at this time was a remark she made when Maria Callas died of a heart attack in her Paris apartment in September. 'Maria never did get what she wanted most – she didn't fight hard enough for the important things,' she said.

Four days later, on 20 September, *The New York Times* revealed another side of Christina's determination at any cost to get what she wanted, when it disclosed the details of her settlement with Jackie. Confirming that the agreement had been reached in June the previous year, a spokesman for the Onassis Foundation told the newspaper: 'Mrs Onassis is a woman who knows how to protect and augment her rights. She took advantage of Christina's wish to become controller of the part of the Onassis estate she was legally entitled to, and asked for her share.' The $26 million lump sum was in addition to the $200,000 a year originally provided for her in Ari's will, it was explained.

The New York Times noted that the settlement represented almost double what Jackie would have received under Ari's will, and seven times what she would have got had he lived to complete the divorce proceedings. But Christina was perfectly satisfied. 'I can live with it,' she told Costa Gratsos, 'if Jackie can.'

—10—

To say that you can love one
person all your life is like saying
that one candle will continue
burning as long as you live

Leo Tolstoy
The Kreutzer Sonata

CHRISTINA FELL IN LOVE EASILY, and her passion was both boundless and brief. She turned away from lovers and husbands, and turned towards others, with a capriciousness that was beginning to worry the Olympic hierachy as well as her family. Her emotional equilibrium, which continued to be achieved only with difficulty and with drugs, made it impossible for anyone to predict her moods, or what or who would take her fancy next.

And *nobody* saw Sergei Kauzov coming.

During one of Christina's many fights with Alexander Andreadis, she had flown to Moscow with Costa Gratsos to try to lease the Russians some of Olympic's surplus bulk carriers. The man she was dealing with was Kauzov, then in charge of the tanker division of Sovfracht, a department of the Soviet Ministry of the Maritime Fleet. They got on well. Although Christina had no recollection of it, Kauzov told her that they had met briefly once before, in Monaco. He reminded her that she had been 'not very nice' to him, and had wanted to know how a Communist party official justified his presence in a town like Monte Carlo – and whose money was he spending? He was not turned off by Christina's capitalist aggression, however, and the talks in Moscow got off to a promising start.

They were still talking in November 1977 when Christina was asked to go to the Sovfracht office in Paris to clarify some points in a deal for the Russians to lease five Olympic tankers on five-year charters. The contract was definitely a feather in Christina's cap and she wanted to 'cross the t's and dot the i's' herself. She was surprised and rather pleased when she arrived at the Russian office, between a *charcuterie* and a cheese shop, on rue des Huissiers in the suburbs of Neuilly-sur-Seine, to discover that the new bureau chief was Sergei Kauzov himself.

Within days they had started an affair.

'In bed he is the best,' she told Florence Grinda, with whom she discussed her seductions in immediate and considerable detail. ('She often made the first move, her approach was very direct,' Florence later described Christina's style.)

Not much taller than Christina, Sergei Kauzov was a slim man with brown hair, thinning at the crown, a gold tooth, and one eye that did not move, the result of a boyhood accident. He was far from handsome, certainly, but it was a very agreeable face and there was a benignity in his smile that Christina trusted. Forty years old (he had a wife, Natalya, and a nine-year-old daughter, Katya, back in Moscow), a graduate of the Moscow Institute of Foreign Languages, a Ministry of State Security officer training school, Kauzov was also a KGB agent. 'So much forbidden fruit in one basket,' Christina would later recall. '*Quelle blague!* Who could resist?' ('She fell in love with the Russian because he *was* such an impossible case. A married man, with a family, he was a challenge,' said Florence Grinda.)

For several months they pursued their romance in small hotels and over dinners *à deux* at Avenue Foch (one word in the press, Sergei had impressed on her, and he would be hauled back to Moscow faster than you could say Feliks Dzerzhinsky). In February, they succeeded in slipping away together to Brazil for Carnival. Christina booked one of the two suites that occupy the whole of the ninth floor of the Copacabaña Palace Hotel. It was wildly romantic. The glorious weather, the throb of the samba, the excitement of the intrigue, became too much for her susceptible imagination. Before Carnival was over the capitalist heiress, one of the richest women in the world, owner of a private jet, a yacht, five homes and an island in the sun, asked Sergei Danyelovich Kauzov, loyal member of the Soviet Communist party, $175-a-week apparatchik and agent of the KGB, to marry her.

The affair was not the big secret that Christina imagined it to be, however. Because of his equivocal background, Kauzov was listed as a 'target alien' by the Service des Renseignements, the French security organization. At the beginning of December, a routine check had turned up her licence plate number among the cars visiting the Sovfracht offices.

A surveillance operation in the following weeks revealed the extent of the relationship. By the time the lovers were taking the Varig flight to Brazil in February both the CIA and British intelligence services had been alerted and were following their progress with keen interest.

Christina had access to the kind of information which, in the hands of Soviet intelligence analysts, could reveal a great deal about Western energy needs and fluctuations. The Russians must have been wetting their lips when they heard about Kauzov's luck, said an MI5 officer in London. In Washington a CIA Soviet expert dismissed the idea that Christina had been set up by the KGB. Kauzov was not the kind of man who would have been expected to seduce her, he said. Their affair was an opportune accident that the KGB was naturally going to exploit.

The next step in the game came a few weeks after they returned from the Rio Carnival: Kauzov was recalled to Moscow. Christina was frantic. He had given her no warning, offered no explanation. She had no way of contacting him in Russia. The people in Sovfracht's Paris bureau would tell her nothing. Angry, distressed, puzzled, she pulled every string she knew to find out what had happened to her lover. Among the people she turned to was David Karr, an old friend of Ari's, who had helped pave the way to Sovfracht's Moscow door. Karr, whose friendship with several important Soviet officials, including Premier Alexei Kosygin's son-in-law Dzherman Gvishiani, deputy chairman of the State Committee for Science and Technology, had brought him to the notice of the CIA, soon came up with Kauzov's home number in Moscow. He told her not to call him through the operator in Paris but to go to London and use the IDD (International Direct Dialling) system that linked London and Moscow. She flew to London at once and called Kauzov's number.

After the strain and mystery of the past weeks she could hardly believe her luck when she heard Kauzov's story. He had been recalled by his Sovfracht chief Nikolai Zuev to run a new tanker division; at first he thought it best if they never saw each other again, but now he realized he missed her very much ... and had asked his wife for a divorce.

During the following weeks she flew to London three times a week to talk to her lover in Moscow. The intrigue was tremendous. Florence Grinda was one of the very few friends in Paris who knew what was going on, and listened in fascination to Christina's plans. 'I don't want this divorce to take forever. I'm going to pay off his wife. It will cost nothing. One hundred thousand dollars is a fortune in Russia. It'll take care of everything,' she said. Later she was contemplating a plot to smuggle Kauzov to the West in one of her tankers; she said she would pay $500,000 to anyone who could ensure his freedom. It seemed to Florence rather extreme, but given Christina's determination and impatience something she would attempt if she had to.

A meeting in Moscow was arranged for May. Christina set off by train from Paris in high hopes. At Moscow's Byelorussia station she was to be met by a man who would take her to Sergei. But the rendezvous was not kept and Christina caught the next train back to Paris. For a week she did not leave Avenue Foch, did not call Kauzov, refused to talk to anyone, and played endlessly the music from *Doctor Zhivago*. Then she pulled herself together, returned to London and called her lover.

This time she heard some remarkable news. Sergei's wife had agreed to a divorce and accepted the financial provisions. He would be free to marry within six weeks – if Christina were prepared to live in Moscow!

She agreed at once.

After a tearful farewell in Paris (at the station she handed the faithful Eleni a parting gift of $200,000 in bills) Christina arrived at the Byelorussia railway station on Sunday, 25 June. Sergei was waiting. He drove her straight to the Intourist Hotel on Gorky Street. Their 'reunion, engagement and the first day of the rest of my life in Russia' (as she later described the scene, at first with emotion, eventually with hilarity) was rapturously consummated in the double bed of her twelfth-floor bedroom overlooking Red Square.

Moscow was not a pleasant place to be in the summer of 1978. An almost continual rain prevented the Russians from flocking to the local river beaches; a dark cloud also hung over East–West relations. Hopes of détente between the United States and the Soviet Union receded as President Jimmy Carter elevated human rights to the level of government policy, and President Leonid Brezhnev responded by cracking down harder than ever on Soviet dissidents. The KGB was quick to arrest and the courts were imposing stricter sentences than ever on so-called political troublemakers. Western correspondents were also in the firing line, attacked in the Soviet press, and frequently summoned to the Foreign Ministry to be reprimanded for writing 'anti-Soviet slanders'.

Christina's arrival in Moscow was a gift to these correspondents, who welcomed the chance to file a few stories that didn't concern dissidents, the KGB or Kremlin politics. The suggestion that she planned to marry a Russian (leaked, like her presence in Moscow, by the CIA, who were hoping to put the skids under her plans with embarrassing publicity) was greeted with disbelief by the Western newsmen. Nevertheless, they treated the story as a twist on *Ninotchka*, the prewar Hollywood romance about serious Russian comrade Greta Garbo falling in love with serious Western capitalist Melvyn Douglas. But it was the darker shades of Le Carré and not the pastel pinks of Lubitsch that Washington and Whitehall perceived. The source of this anxiety was a French intelligence tip that Christina had been persuaded to open an office in Moscow – with Kauzov, who had inexplicably suddenly quit his job with Sovfracht, running it. 'If the Onassis tanker fleet were to fall under Soviet influence, the men in the Kremlin would have much more than a propaganda coup,' a Western shipping analyst pointed out the potential strategic threat.

When the consequences were spelled out to Costa Gratsos by State Department officials in Washington, the Onassis veteran flew immediately to Moscow. In Christina's suite at the Intourist Hotel he presented all the facts – including Sergei Kauzov's rank in the KGB. He hoped that she would at least reconsider her plans to marry the Russian, he said. She told him that she would think it over.

She continued to react indignantly when newsmen put the marriage rumours to her. She was simply a tourist, she said. Talk of marriage was absolutely preposterous ... untrue ... stupid ... a lie. But at the beginning of July a rumour went through the Western correspondents' community that the wedding was set for the tenth. The source was the Greek Embassy, which would have to be represented at any Soviet wedding of such a prominent national. It was not what the newsmen wanted to hear, for that was the date when two of the Soviet Union's best-known dissidents, Anatoly Scharansky and Alexander Ginsburg, were to go on trial. It seemed possible that the KGB was attempting to use her wedding as a diversion from the trials. But the tenth came and went without incident. 'You see, I told you, these stories are absolute rubbish,' she said triumphantly.

But the speculation did not go away, nor was it rife only in Moscow.

In Athens, her aunts were appalled, anxious and querulous. Artemis was in a punitive frame of mind; she wanted her niece psychiatrically examined, sure that she would be certified mad.

When Alexander Andreadis heard the rumours from Russia he telephoned Stavros Niarchos. 'Mr Niarchos, you must stop her going through with this. It's madness, please talk to her,' he pleaded. Niarchos asked why Andreadis imagined she would listen to him. Andreadis said that Christina respected him and would take notice of his opinion. Niarchos said, 'Well, I don't think she will. She paid no attention when I told her not to marry you!'

On 27 July, Christina summoned English journalist Denis Blewett to her Intourist suite and, with Sergei Kauzov at her side (in a well-cut blue suit, blue shirt, and black tie), named the day: 1 August. In a front-page world scoop in the London *Daily Mail*, Blewett reported that she also intended to make her home in the Soviet Union, and to start a family straight away. 'I expect my child to be born here, where else?' she said.

But amid the implausibility permissible in love stories – they would live with Sergei's mother until they could buy a cooperative apartment ('I've had luxuries for so long that to go without won't be such a problem; the world knows I haven't had much happiness until now; we want to be left in peace'), Sergei didn't have a job and had no idea what he wanted to do next – Christina said very deliberately: 'I want the world to know – and this is very important – that the Onassis business will continue to be run by my father's old associates. There will be no changes. All this speculation I have read about the headquarters being moved to Moscow is quite wrong.'

It was a victory for the West; it was also a hint that Christina was already losing some of her entrancement with Russia. Certainly the story she was telling to the world was not the story she was telling to her friends. The idea of living with her sixty-five-year-old mother-in-law Mariya Sergeyevna depressed her immeasurably. The second-floor apartment, on an estate built in the 1950s on the outskirts of Moscow, contained two small bedrooms, a meagrely furnished sitting room, kitchen (with a refrigerator but no washing machine or dishwasher) and one tiny bathroom. ('It's not exactly the Winter Palace,' she summed it up neatly to a Paris friend.)

Not only had 'Lara's Theme' lost its charm but her feelings for Sergei had taken a ninety-degree turn. A few days before the wedding, she told Florence Grinda, 'I'm no longer in love with Sergei, but I can't let him down. I owe that much to him. It's gone too far to stop now ... but there certainly won't be any children!'

It was a fine day for the wedding, held in the former mansion of Prince Felix Yussupov (who had been the richest man in Russia in 1918), which the Bolsheviks had turned into Moscow's number one Palace of Weddings. The $2.15 ceremony, held in an oak-panelled room dominated by portraits of Brezhnev and Lenin, and a faded mosaic of the hammer and sickle, lasted seven minutes. Instead of the well-worn record of Tchaikovsky's *Romeo and Juliet*, a string quartet (optional extra) played Mendelssohn as Christina, in a simple cotton dress patterned with tiny red and white flowers, entered the room on the arm of Sergei. On a signal from Mrs Klara Yemshekova, a state official and academic specialist on marriage, they stopped ten feet from her desk. 'The executive committee of the Soviet of Working People's Deputies of the City of Moscow has empowered me to register your marriage.' Mrs Yemshekova went on to describe the solemnity of marriage – 'the most important and honourable event in your lives' – and of the Soviet government's interest in its success. 'You will not achieve happiness without working at it,' she told them. 'You must not only love each other, marriage is more than that. You must be attentive, kind and generous to each other, then your love will grow and flourish.' She had a special word for Comrade Sergei: 'Wherever you live, do not forget your Soviet Motherland.' The ceremony was attended by eight guests, none of whom was from the bride's side. Christina was accompanied by John Fotopoulos, the first secretary of the Greek Embassy. Sergei's friend Stefan Stephanov was best man. '*Da*,' Christina replied quickly when Mrs Yemshekova asked if they accepted each other. '*Da*,' repeated Sergei. They exchanged gold rings. Mrs Yemshekova gave them permission to congratulate each other. They kissed each other lightly on the cheek. The string quartet struck up Mendelssohn's 'Wedding March' as the bride and groom brushed past the next couple on the marital conveyor belt, Moscow-style.

Outside they were besieged by Western journalists, photographers and television crews. Christina clutched her small bouquet of white roses and scowled at the crush. Kauzov, now $50,000 a year richer under the terms of Ari's will, shouted at the mob in Russian and English to clear off and leave his wife alone. With difficulty he got Christina and his mother into his brown Volga sedan, from which the windscreen wipers had been removed to thwart thieves while they were inside the Wedding Palace. A handful of bemused Russians watched as he drove through the crowd of reporters and cameramen. There are no gossip columns in the Soviet Union; not a word about Christina and Sergei had appeared in the Russian newspapers. To Soviet editors she was a nonperson; the story of Kauzov's sudden good fortune was not considered newsworthy at all. In a sense it was fortunate for Kauzov since, like his own mother, few if any of the citizens who watched the events that day would have respected a comrade who had abandoned his wife and child for the love of a Western heiress.

But he would soon discover how wayward that love could be. A Siberian honeymoon on the shores of Lake Baikal had been planned, but it never happened. Four days after the ceremony, her bouquet of roses still fresh in the vase on her mother-in-law's mantelpiece, the bride flew back to Greece – alone. Aunt Artemis greeted her with the words, 'How could you love a godless man?' Christina refrained from informing her that she no longer did (that would have led to too many recriminations) but while Kauzov was kept busy explaining to newsmen in Moscow that his bride had been called to Athens on urgent business, she was being photographed sunbathing by the pool of her aunt's seaside villa.

'I'm not sure when she will return, but she will return,' Kauzov answered doggedly when he was told that his wife had left Athens – and gone to Skorpios, with a group of friends. Mariya Sergeyevna was also puzzled by her new daughter-in-law's erratic behaviour. 'She has been calling Sergei twice a day. These calls prove she is crazily in love with my son,' she said.

On Skorpios her friends were just as puzzled. 'Don't you miss Moscow?' a guest asked drily. She said that she missed her friends and her private plane infinitely more. She was particularly mad at the bureaucrats who had refused to allocate her airspace when she wanted to use her own plane for the honeymoon. But surrounded by her old friends on her island, her anger was forgotten. Skorpios was where she always ran to when things became too difficult for her in the real world. 'On Skorpios she is Queen Christina – I've seen peasants literally fall on their knees to kiss her hand,' said Paris friend Jean-Pierre de Lucovich. Another friend who had spent summers on the island said, 'Only on Skorpios does she feel free to dance on tables if that's the mood she is in. It is where she is most like Ari, where you see the real Christina and hear what she really thinks.' Sitting around one evening, they began to play the what-if game and Christina said: 'What if Alexander had not been killed?' Her friends were stunned. How do you answer a question like that? It was Christina herself who came up with the answer. 'I suppose I wouldn't have felt the burden of being an Onassis so heavily. I would have been freer – but I wouldn't have been completely born,' she said.

On 10 August, she flew to London with nothing but business in mind. At lunch with the directors of British Petroleum, one of Olympic's most important customers, they were joined by a Foreign Office minister, whose presence, according to one oil executive, had 'been ordained at a high political level'. During this lunch in the boardroom at Britannic House, BP's headquarters in the City of London, the minister advised her that the anti-communist Saudis were convinced that a KGB man was now 'profoundly influencing' Olympic Maritime affairs. If this was so, and was not corrected immediately, he said the Saudis would not renew their charters. This news shook Christina badly. More than 85 per cent of Olympic's tanker trade involved the transportation of Saudi Arabian oil.

As she left that evening to take her Learjet back to Athens she looked drained and deeply worried. 'Not for all the tea in China would I want a daughter of mine to be in that young woman's shoes right now,' a senior BP man told a colleague. Her anxious state of mind after the day of intense talks with the British oil men – all of them pressing her to heed the minister's warning, or to abandon Moscow altogether – was not helped by an intelligence-inspired tip-off that in her absence Sergei was spending his nights with his former wife, Natalya. Christina called him several times that evening from her London apartment, and from Heathrow; he was not at home. ('When she called yesterday, Sergei was not here ... she seemed worried as to where he had gone,' her mother-in-law confided to the press.) Christina finally got through to him from Athens. 'Are you still in love with your wife?' she angrily demanded. 'Of course I am, and I want you to come back soon,' Sergei told her smoothly.

Christina returned to Moscow on 13 August. For the first time she perceived the marriage as a direct and profound threat to the Onassis empire. She knew exactly what she had to do; it happened to be what she had wanted to do all along, but she had to tread carefully if she was not going to appear a laughing-stock, and if she was not going to humiliate Sergei. She sent a message to the Saudis assuring them that Olympic Maritime would 'take all steps necessary to deal with the problem' that was causing them concern. She figured it would take six months to extricate herself from the Moscow mess.

Publicly she still refused to accept that Sergei had been working for Russian intelligence. Her pride would not permit it. But every move she made from the day she returned from London in August was a move towards her goal of ending the marriage and quitting Moscow with as much dignity and speed as she could muster.

Meanwhile, she would make the best of what she had. What she had very quickly was a seven-room mansion apartment in midtown Moscow, proving that Sergei had pull with *somebody* who could do special favours in that town. Other perks included an import licence for her Mercedes limousine, permission to employ a chauffeur, a permit for Atalanta Politis to decorate the new apartment. She learned how to use her hard currency to buy the special certificate roubles to shop in the Beryozka stores for the luxury Western goods reserved for foreigners and privileged Soviets. Life in Moscow isn't so bad at all, she spent tens of thousands of dollars on telephone calls to assure friends in the West. But she was lonely, and the calls always ended in pleas for them to visit her. Moscow is so exciting, she would tempt them. Once, she said, she was stopped in her car and questioned by the police about a fridge that was strapped to the roof. Objecting to their *tone* (her attempts to learn Russian never got beyond 'seventeen expletives'), she told her driver to put his foot down and they 'escaped at great speed'.

She could hide her loneliness, and she could even hide her sense of oppression in Moscow (Sergei's new job as an English teacher at Moscow's Higher Trade Union School wasn't much fun either), but she could not hide the fact that she was getting fat. She had put on over fourteen pounds in a few months, and was now heavier than she had ever been. She blamed the Russian Pepsi-Cola (her beloved Coke was not available) and caviar. When she flew to Switzerland, ostensibly to see her gynaecologist, rumours started that she was pregnant. She did not deny the rumours, even when they were printed as facts in the press; she used them to excuse her increasingly frequent trips to the West.

Eleven weeks after the Wedding Palace ceremony, Christina privately confided to her husband that her Russian odyssey was over and the clock was also running on their marriage. 'He took it calmly – he wants to leave Russia too!' Christina told Costa Gratsos in Paris in October. The fly in the ointment was that Sergei wanted his mother to join him in the West; he pleaded with Christina to keep the Moscow apartment and delay any talk of divorce until Mariya was safely out of the country. The plot from this moment had the elements of an old-fashioned cold war romantic thriller. ('When Mariya gets out I get out,' was how Christina put the dilemma to Gratsos, who had the tricky job of explaining the situation to the Saudis.)

Christina spent Christmas in St Moritz; Sergei remained in Moscow with mother. In the New Year they met in Paris, and Christina appeared genuinely pleased to see him. 'She still liked Sergei, she wanted to sleep with him, she just didn't want to be married to him,' said one Paris friend. He gave her a red cocker spaniel which she named Yuri, after a character in *Doctor Zhivago*. (She loved Yuri, but it was Sergei the neighbours saw walking and toilet-training it on Avenue Foch.)

But being married to a Russian schoolteacher who dutifully walks your cocker spaniel every morning is not in the same class as having a Russian spy slipping out of your boudoir each dawn. Clearly Sergei had lost something in translation. 'When we go to dinners, nobody talks to him, nobody finds him *chic*,' she complained to Florence Grinda, who was astonished at Christina's attitude.

'I said to her, "Christina, you can be so clever and so stupid! Can't you see, he is a fascinating man. All this stuff about the KGB . . . people are dying to meet him. Don't say he isn't *chic* just because he has no small talk!" She simply couldn't see that at all,' said Florence, who rather liked Sergei and found him a decent human being too.

Christina was not convinced. And although she kept her promise to keep up the charade of a happy marriage until her mother-in-law got to the West, the strain on her was considerable. (Instead of taking off weight, she continued to put it on. Taki Theodoracopulos nicknamed her 'Thunderthighs' after seeing a picture of her by aunt Artemis's pool.) In St Moritz at Easter she abandoned Sergei on the nursery slopes, just as she had abandoned Alexander Andreadis before him, while she went off with the George Livanos crowd.

In June, Maria Niarchos married Alix Chevassus, another pharmaceutical heir. To celebrate the occasion, Stavros gave a $500,000 ball for nine hundred guests at Lisieux, his Normandy château. It was the sort of party Christina thrived on. Guests included Princess Caroline of Monaco, the Aga Khan and his beautiful British-born wife Sally, and practically every grand name in Greek shipping and European aristocracy (as well as Luis Basualdo, now divorced from Viscount Cowdray's daughter Lucy, and dating a tall English beauty named Clare Lawman). 'Sergei will be bored silly, and I will have the time of my life,' she told Florence Grinda. But with his quiet charm, his reputation as a spy and as a lover, Sergei found no difficulty in fending for himself among the mega-rich.

That summer, even while she prepared to shed Sergei and continued to work on the fine print of the financial settlement, Christina decided that a grand first anniversary party on Skorpios would be jolly. She invited Princess Caroline, and her husband of a year, Philippe Junot, former Beatle Ringo Starr, and a bunch of her closest friends from Paris. It was not Sergei's crowd but he was happy to let Christina play *La Reina*, a role he knew she relished.

And there were compensations. To help him get started on his own in the shipping business she had given him an 18,000-ton bulk carrier which she bought for $3.5 million. And two months after that gift, she bought him a 60,000-ton tanker for $4 million.

On 5 November 1979, with his mother safely established in England, and himself living in a $600-a-week apartment off Piccadilly (and taking tea each afternoon at Fortnum and Mason), it was revealed in Athens that the couple were seeking a divorce. 'The reports in the Greek newspapers are wicked and malicious,' Christina replied at once. But a month later, after a solo spree in New York, where she spent every night with a different escort at the nightclub Studio 54, she announced that divorce proceedings had begun on the grounds of irreconcilable differences.

—11—

*I like you. I love you. I want you
all the time, so please wire back
that you'll be my valentine*

Western Union
Form No. 2

As she passed her thirtieth birthday and put behind her a decade in which she lost her whole family, became the most famous heiress in the world, and saw her three marriages fail, Christina Onassis faced up to the future and 'the challenge of remaking my life'. Between her birthday, on 11 December (celebrated at Maxim's, minus her latest escort, perfume heir Yvon Coty: 'All he likes from me is a blow-job,' she said, striking his name firmly off the invitation list. 'He can go screw himself!'), and the New Year, she earnestly set about clearing the decks.

She rehired Eleni – and took back the $200,000 parting gift she had given her faithful maid at the emotional farewell scene when she was Moscow-bound in June. She invited Hubert Michard-Pelissier and his sisters Florence (Grinda) and Caroline to spend Christmas with her at the Villa Cristal. But even that interlude had a business purpose. A lawyer like his late father, Hubert was preparing Christina's divorce petition and the villa was conveniently close to Samaden, the town down the valley from St Moritz, where the papers were to be field in the New Year. Even the possibility that she was having a little fling with Hubert was scotched by Florence: 'Lovers, no. Best friends, of course.' In Christina's own words: 'I have put a moratorium on sex.'

Not that Christina was all business. she was photographed with Philippe Junot, his marriage to Princess Caroline on the rocks; and linked with forty-year-old polo player Jean-Jacques Cornet-Epinet. She continued to take uncomplicated and perhaps congenital pleasure in spending money on her favourite people. Luis Basualdo had turned up in St Moritz (he was recovering from a polo injury to his back at the ever-accommodating Palace Hotel). And he and Hubert got in plenty of skiing with Christina, using her helicopter to reach the highest runs sometimes a dozen times a day; local residents complained constantly about the noise. By night she entertained at home, where Alberto and Marina Dodero, Peugeot PR director Jean Yturbe and his heiress wife Sandy Bemberg had joined her other houseguests. To celebrate the New Year, she took over the Chesa Veglia restaurant for a dinner party for seventy, including the Aga Khan and his wife Sally, Philippe Niarchos and his girlfriend Manuella Papatakis (daughter of French film actress Anouk Aimée), Spyros Niarchos, Rudolf Nureyev, Gianni Agnelli and Prince Alexander of Yugoslavia.

Christina's moratorium on sex had loosened considerably by February when in the darkness of the King's Club she encountered Nicky Mavroleon. He was tall, slim, and his dark brown hair curled naturally; at twenty-one, he was almost cartoonishly handsome. Christina ignored him for about two and a quarter minutes, then invited him to dance.

Totally oblivious to Sir Gordon White, Bertil Kalen, Silvana Faccini, Hans and Milana Furstenburg, Peter Bemberg, Laura Rossi and the rest of their friends on hand that night, Christina and Nicky remained so unconscionably entwined that the tactful membrane that remains between even the most passionate dancers might have ceased to exist at all.

Still enjoying Christina's patronage, and the daily use of her chopper ('And why not? she has the daily use of his,' was a joke around King's), Luis Basualdo became dismayed as he watched Mavroleon being installed in her affections. Later he recalled the sacrifices he made to stay close to her at that time; sometimes, he said, he had to swallow up to fifteen aspirins to relieve the pain in his back before he could ski with her. 'And I had to ski with her to be in power, to be there, to render opinions in her house,' he explained the subtle demands placed on men like himself in the lives of women like Christina.

At dawn, clutching the charming youth firmly by the hand, Christina returned to the Villa Cristal. The clamorous cries of ecstasy and discovery coming from her bedroom for the rest of that morning were unrelenting. Marina Dodero, who had been startled into wakefulness by the activity in the adjoining room, was impressed; she had thought Christina had worn herself out dancing.

Nicky Mavroleon was unlike any of Christina's previous lovers or husbands. Educated at Eton, nine years younger than Christina, he was the son of an Anglicized Greek shipping millionaire and a Mexican mother. His parents had been divorced for some years and his father's second marriage, to Somerset Maugham's granddaughter Camilla, was also breaking up. Nicky had no regular job, an unsettled home life and an inadequate allowance from his father. Christina listened to his story with grave concern. It was clear to her, if not yet to Nicky, that an affair was on the cards. Not wishing to have another impoverished lover on her hands, and already more than a little in love with him, she put Nicky on the Olympic payroll and loaned him $50,000 to cover his immediate commitments.

The affair took off and quickly became the talk of St Moritz. But when the couple moved to Paris in March, young Nicky began to feel uneasy with the arrangement he found himself saddled with. His pride dictated that he did not want to be seen living with – and off – a rich woman. His father, who had moved from London to tax exile in Switzerland, urged him to break off the liaison before he became a complete wastrel and idler. But with her cunning loan, Christina had a hold over her unwilling lover and did not hesitate to pull the strings whenever he tried to discuss the possible careers that were open to a man with his good connections.

But after three months of intense socializing and some emotional ups and downs with her young, and, in her view, ungrateful lover, Christina confided to friends that she felt 'almost suicidal'. She had been seeing a psychiatrist three times a week for a year in Paris but was not happy with her progress. She consulted her doctor in New York. He suspected acute depression and invited her to New York for diagnostic observation and rest. She was booked into the Lennox Hill Hospital. Basualdo, who had gone to New York from St Moritz, couldn't believe his luck when Christina turned up not only in the same city but a few blocks from Mortimer's, the restaurant where he lunched every day. Keen to renew their close friendship (he admitted that his 'nose had been put out of joint' by Mavroleon's occupation of Avenue Foch), he sat with her for hours every single day, listening to her woes, trying to cheer her up with his outrageous stories and schemes.

Another attentive caller, one of the few close friends who knew of Christina's hospitalization, was Marina Dodero. But Marina had her own problems, and priorities. Her father was on the verge of bankruptcy, and she herself was suicidal. According to the story Christina told Basualdo, she agreed to lend the Doderos $4 million interest-free for four years. 'Now go home to Buenos Aires. I'm very tired and depressed and I don't want to see anyone,' she told her grateful friend. Instead of returning to Argentina, Christina learned later, Marina hung around New York until it was confirmed that the money had been deposited in the Doderos' Swiss account. 'That irritated Christina tremendously, having her word doubted. But she said, "Now I've got a couple for life." So whenever there was an argument between them she said, "Goddamit, you owe me *four million*, how dare you!" It was a lot of money just to get a couple of friends to dance to your tune. I certainly never thought the money would be repaid, and neither did Christina's people in Monte Carlo,' said Basualdo.

After three weeks Christina declared herself well again, discharged herself from Lennox Hill and optimistically returned to 'the challenge of remaking my life'. Following a week of talks with her Olympic uncles in New York, the ageing Costa Gratsos – her father's oldest, closest friend and wisest advisor – agreed to step down in her favour. Christina had been especially critical of Gratsos's alleged offer to Muhammad Ali of a 1 per cent commission – 'worth $25 billion,' the former heavyweight boxing champion bragged – if Ali could effect an introduction to Libyan leader Colonel Muammar Gaddafi, leading to a deal to transport and refine Libyan oil. Costa Gratsos had played an important part in the creation of the Onassis fortune and he understood better than anyone the winner-take-all philosophy Ari had infused into his daughter. 'When she began using the Ali business as an excuse to attack me personally, I knew it was time for me to go,' he said shortly before his death in December 1981. 'I wished her only good luck,' he said.

'We all felt that Christina needed to find the emotional stability she had been missing for so long,' Olympic lawyer Stelios Papadimitriou explained when he announced her total takeover of the company. 'The business had inevitably faced complications as a result. But now, after long discussions with Christina, she has convinced us that she is anxious to take on the task and prove herself. She is quite capable of coping. After all, she has been trained in the job for seven years.'

But the new-found emotional stability that had impressed Papa-dimitriou and some of her uncles in New York (who knew nothing of her sojourn at Lennox Hill) immediately came under renewed pressure when she returned to Paris and Nicky Mavroleon told her that he did not intend to join the Skorpios circus that summer.

In a misguided attempt to 'punish' her young lover, Christina flew in June to La Jolla for a vacation with Sergei Kauzov. It was just a month since their Swiss divorce, and followed some extremely unflattering comments he had made about her to an Italian journalist ('I married Christina for two reasons. Because she asked me and because I liked her. Russians like fat women and Christina is fat).' But her evident affection for Sergei in Southern California astonished everybody, including the grateful and devoted Doderos who had accompanied them on the trip, rejoicing that the Tchomlekdjoglou business had been saved by Christina's generosity.

The ploy to make Nicky jealous was not successful, and Christina returned to Paris at the end of June as depressed as she had been when she was admitted to Lennox Hill in the spring. But when once again she bumped into Luis Basualdo and his English girlfriend, Clare Lawman, late one evening in the Relais Plaza restaurant at the Plaza Athenée Hotel she brightened up considerably, and before the evening was over she had invited them both to Skorpios for the whole summer. 'You always cheer me up, Sosita,' she said, recalling an old nickname. 'I'm so lucky to have walked into this restaurant this evening.'

It was also a fortunate encounter for Luis, who was running low on funds after collecting only a modest £200,000 payoff from Lord Cowdray following his divorce from the viscount's daughter Lucy. Indeed, Luis's finances had reached such a parlous state that he usually restricted Clare to one course at dinner. But that particular night, after an especially good bottle of wine, Luis was feeling 'cute and sweet, and I let Clare have an ice cream, which delayed us for an extra five minutes, and in those five minutes Christina walked in and we got the invitation to Skorpios,' he later admired the vagaries of fate.

It was a typical summer on the island. Luis and Clare were billeted in the Pink House, which, because of its unhappy associations with Jackie, Christina refused to use herself. In the villas attached to the main house were the Yturbes, Henri de Castellane and his wife Atalanta Politis, Florence Grinda, a couple of French decorators (known as 'the poosties', which Christina claimed was Greek for gays), and the ubiquitous Doderos. This nucleus was relieved by an ebb and flow from the corners of Europe. There were three hard floodlit tennis courts

(Christina seldom played herself), an Olympic-size pool, dozens of mini-mokes, and several speedboats. Topless bathing was strictly forbidden (even the smallest toddlers running naked on the beach had to be covered when Christina came into view). Christina's residence, a marble pavilion, on the terrace of which breakfast was served every morning from 10 a.m., overlooked the children's beach. Lunch was at 5 p.m. and dinner began at around 11 p.m. (except when uncle George Livanos came for a brief stay with Sunbun, now the Duke of Marlborough, and meals were taken with uncommon punctuality at 1.30 p.m. and 9 p.m.) followed by the latest movie from Paris. Christina seldom appeared before three in the afternoon, and would breakfast on a chocolate croissant and a Diet Coke, during which, with great absorption, she prepared a list of activities for the following day. Favoured guests were treated to a helicopter ride around the island or to Corfu, thirty minutes away. Others were permitted a trip on the motorlaunch, *Alexander*. There were half a dozen jetskis available (it took fifteen minutes on a calm sea to reach the mainland) and the allotment of activities defined those who were in and out of Christina's favour. After the film show – which, if the movie bored her, she would terminate in midscene: 'she never gave a fuck if anyone else wanted to keep watching,' said Basualdo – Christina might get an urge to go dancing. There was a disco on the nearby island of Nidri. If it had closed for the night, Christina, clutching her own supply of Cokes, would order it to start up again. The proprietors were well rewarded and looked forward to her patronage.

Always quixotic to her circle, Christina had taken an unusual fancy to Florence Grinda's pet dog, a small black mongrel called Pongo. And Pongo seemed fond of Christina. One afternoon, after Pongo had given her a particularly affectionate welcome, Christina offered to buy him from her friend for $1,000. Florence declined the offer. Christina became obsessed with the idea of owning Pongo and each day the offer went up. When the bidding reached $50,000, Florence said: 'Christina, I know you genuinely adore Pongo, and I think he truly loves you. But he belongs to my daughter. So I cannot let you have him.' Christina pleaded with her to consult her daughter Geraldine, who was in Paris. 'Tell her,' she said, 'I will pay $100,000 but no more.' Florence called her daughter and explained the interesting situation. Accept, said the wise child. 'She will get fed up with him in a few days and give him back to us for nothing.' The following day, before they could conclude the deal,

Christina, who was very heavy indeed at this point, inadvertently sat on Pongo. After that, whenever she came into the room, the little dog would snarl and bare his teeth at her. She never mentioned the deal again.

After a couple of weeks Luis Basualdo became bored and more than a little annoyed at being ignored by his former lover. He was also extremely fed up with the island rule that nobody went to bed until Christina had gone to bed, whatever ungodly hour that might be. Even the certainty of free and regular meals could not make up for this damage to his pride, or compensate for his loss of sleep. Sandy Yturbe was having similar feelings and the two of them agreed to leave the island and continue, with their companions, their vacation elsewhere.

At the end of one extremely long evening, during which Christina had again ignored him completely, Basualdo told her straight out: 'Look here, Christina, enough is enough. I won't be treated like shit. You've hardly spoken a word to Clare and me the whole time we've been here. We're leaving in the morning.'

However divided opinion might be on the question of Luis Basualdo's ethics as a lover or a husband, he certainly came to Skorpios with a reputation for devotion and long service to Christina. Christina, who knew this better than anyone, began to cry and said she did not want him to leave. She had already worked out a plan to enable him to stay with her for ever, she told him with what might have been sudden impulse or considered conviction. 'I don't expect you to stay with me out of pure friendship. My doctors have told me that I should have security, I should have someone with me all the time, I want you and little Clare to stay with me, and I will pay you,' she said.

Basualdo's Indian eyes must have narrowed when he heard this. 'No way, Christina,' he remembers the conversation. 'You're my friend, we've known each other for almost eleven years. You will never have to pay me to be your friend.'

Christina was adamant. 'Luis, please, my doctor insists I have a regular companion. I want *you*. It is only right that you should be paid.' Basualdo allowed himself slowly and apparently with great reluctance to be persuaded. 'If your doctor insists, if it makes you feel better, if it will help you ... okay, I'll take some money, I don't care,' he remembers the scene as Christina pressed on him the duty of sparing her loneliness. 'How much do you have in mind?' he asked.

She said, 'How about twenty or thirty thousand dollars a month?'

'And I said, "I suppose thirty thousand will do, if it helps you." You see, I knew she wanted to own me. She wanted to possess me. For that I was to be her companion all the time, be constantly at her disposal, be her bodyguard, twenty-four hours a day I would be there, *hers*,' he said with the equanimity of a man who understands the very rich, who knows that men like himself will always be discarded by people like Christina when they no longer fulfil a purpose. 'I insisted that Clare was part of the deal, with a dress allowance, and everything taken care of,' Basualdo recalled the deal struck on Skorpios.

When news of the appointment reached the Onassis office in Monte Carlo there was disbelief and anger – $360,000 a year, all expenses paid ('the only time he has to put his hand in his pocket is to scratch his balls,' said one Olympic man) was more than some of the most senior executives were paid. When a journalist enquired about the latest addition to Christina's staff, a terse statement was issued: 'Mr Luis Basualdo is working for Miss Onassis as her "*compagnon*", as we say in French. That means a male companion. His duties are to accompany her to shows, dinners or concerts, and attend to her needs.'

The eventful summer on Skorpios over, Christina returned to Avenue Foch, where Basualdo and little Clare (Christina was punctilious about the 'little') were installed in a first-floor apartment. Still resenting Nicky Mavroleon's refusal to dance attendance on Skorpios, still purporting to be in love with him, she could think of little else but how to make him toe the Onassis line. She threatened to call in his $50,000 loan, obviously a heavy burden of conscience on a young man of twenty-one. But Nicky, training to be a helicopter pilot in England, refused to be intimidated or called to heel in Paris.

Christina's next move was extraordinary, even by her own extra-ordinary standards. She announced that she was pregnant, and Nicky Mavroleon was the father. He was astonished by her claim, and on 10 October flew to Paris to discuss the situation with her face to face. He told her that he was making arrangements to return her $50,000 within weeks, and that there was no possibility of marriage. It was not what Christina had expected to hear at all. She broke down, and sobbingly admitted that she had invented the story of a baby to win him back.

Whatever sympathy Nicky felt for Christina he kept to himself. He told the London *Daily Mail*: 'Although she may look a bit overweight, she's not pregnant. I admit that if there was a child, there is a possibility of me being the father – but there is no child.' Her friends felt sorry for her. 'It wasn't tragic, but she made a fool of herself,' Florence Grinda summed up the feeling in her crowd.

But Nicky's public rejection and his exposure of her lie – both widely reported in the gossip columns and magazines Christina loved best – had deeply humiliated her, and she was hurt and perplexed. Basualdo had never seen her in such despair. She looked a mess. She had again stopped brushing her teeth, did nothing with her hair, and her weight had ballooned to 180 pounds. Basualdo began to earn his salary as she alternately wept and fantasized incoherently about marrying Mavroleon, and sat in a drugged silence staring at the wall, sometimes until five o'clock in the morning, before allowing him and little Clare to put her to bed.

Basualdo knew that she was in deep psychological trouble. He also knew she was on drugs (in addition to the antidepressant shots she continued to get from her nurse, Veronique), but only now did he discover to what extent. She was back on amphetamines, and they were stronger than ever. She called them 'my black beauties'; they were prescribed by a gynaecologist in New York. There were two kinds: the stronger ones she called *mavro mavro* ('black black', in Greek); and the slightly milder kind *mavro aspro* ('black white'). Basualdo came to dread '*mavro mavro* time'. They put Christina into a hyperactive state that increased the stress, as well as the workload, on him and on little Clare.

When she was high she wanted to dance all night. She never wanted the music to stop. The moment she felt she was coming down, she popped another *mavro mavro*. 'I would dance with her for half an hour, then Clare would dance with her for half an hour. Clare got blisters on her feet,' Basualdo later recalled the marathon *mavro mavro* nights in the clubs of Paris. Her behaviour became erratic in other ways too. She would leave Avenue Foch only after dark. White-faced, drugged and disoriented, but with Basualdo always by her side, she liked to roam through the Paris Metro, and go slumming in the low-life dives of Montparnasse and other sleazy rundown *arrondissements*.

Summoned to her bedroom one morning when she could not sleep, even after her regular fistful of barbiturates, Basualdo was horrified to find that she had defecated in the sheets and remained lying in the mess.

He was now convinced that she was not only having a mental breakdown but was also on the edge of really going under. He was scared of the strain her bloated, souped-up body was putting on her heart. 'What are we going to do with her?' he asked Clare. 'She doesn't want to live and she doesn't want to die.'

But the crisis – 'my Mavroleon madness,' she later called it, as if it had been no more than a romantic interlude – began to recede after a couple of months. Abetted by Eleni, Basualdo had succeeded in replacing nearly half of her nine bedtime barbiturates with placebos. She appeared relatively stabilized when she and her growing entourage (Eleni, Basualdo, little Clare, the Doderos and her nurse, Veronique) returned to the Villa Cristal for Christmas and the New Year celebrations.

Although she had not kicked her 'black beauty' habit, she had worked out a regime for herself where she abstained completely for one day in three. 'On the third day she was always very agitated and wanted to be doing something, going somewhere,' says Basualdo. 'We would go for long walks, up and down the mountains; she was terribly strong. But often we would take the plane and go to Vienna, or to Venice. We flew to Venice five times. If we missed Samaden [the airport for St Moritz], which closed at five, we would stay the night at the Cipriani, or the Gritti Palace.'

Basualdo was always pleased for an opportunity to stay in a hotel with little Clare since Christina had forbidden them to make love in the Villa Cristal. 'She didn't like anyone making love in her house. She used to get the maids to inspect the sheets every morning. The Doderos wouldn't dare defy her wishes, but Clare and I weren't always so obedient. If the maids found anything suspicious, they called Eleni, who told Christina, and we were moved out of the villa to a $500-a-day suite at the Palace, suite 61. Christina liked Clare, they got on well together most of the time, but she resented her too. Clare was very skinny and beautiful and Christina hated the fact that we made love every day. She complained that Clare was too physical.' (Christina's own physical demands on Basualdo had not faded away; he continued to be summoned to her bedroom to prove his worth.)

Christina's life was assuming a pattern which she was to keep. From Christmas until the end of March she would stay in St Moritz, using her plane to fly in friends and occasionally fly herself out if bad weather or tedium set in. From Easter until June she was based at Avenue Foch, followed by a short break in La Jolla, the Californian resort she had learned to love with Joe Bolker. Skorpios was home for July and August, with a steady stream of thirty or forty friends coming and going. In the fall it was back to Paris, with occasional forays to London, where she took a suite at the Hilton Hotel in Park Lane.

Although it was apparent that Stelio Papadimitriou was no longer depending on Christina to run Olympic, she still had plenty on her plate as 1982 began. The Greek government was demanding $50 million in taxes; she protested that the Onassis estate consisted of shares in companies based in Panama, and she owed the Greek government nothing. The imbroglio did not stop her becoming the first woman to be elected to the board of the Greek Union of Shipowners. Although this was rather a formality (ownership of 500 tons of shipping equalled one vote; Christina's forty-six ships had a tonnage in excess of five million) she enjoyed being acknowledged as a leading player of the game. She even enjoyed being made the Union's Director of International Public Relations, a title of exceptional irrelevance.

She had got over Nicky Mavroleon, and her most attentive lover was again Sergei Kauzov, who now had an interest in ten ships, and used 88 Avenue Foch as his Paris base. 'It's an open divorce,' Christina told anyone who had the temerity to express surprise at her unusual arrangement with her ex-husband. Sergei accepted when she asked him to spend a couple of weeks with her in the house she had rented at La Jolla Beach and Tennis Club in June. He flew to California from London. Christina flew from Paris with Basualdo, little Clare and the nurse Veronique. The Doderos (Marina was pregnant with their second child) were coming from Buenos Aires. But at Los Angeles International it was discovered that Veronique did not have a valid US visa and the Immigration officials refused to let her in. It took several hours before Olympic executives in New York tracked down the right man in Washington to give approval for the nurse to enter the country.

When the group finally arrived at the house in La Jolla it was 3 a.m. Sergei was fast asleep in Christina's bed. Exhausted by the long flight from Paris, still in a foul temper over the delay in Immigration, the sight of the Russian sleeping in her bed was the last straw. 'She went crazy,' says Basualdo. 'She threw him out of the house on the spot, and threw his clothes after him.'

Sergei moved into a room at the clubhouse and made himself scarce.

Sightings were reported to Christina, and he was difficult to miss: he had taken to wearing a Popeye cap and covering his body with a yoghurt cream to prevent sunburning on the beach. It did not protect him from the heat he continued to get from his ex-wife. 'It's too embarrassing to be seen with him,' she told Basualdo, who was not displeased to see the only other regular man in her life so discomfited. 'Keep him away from me,' she said as she went about her meetings with executives who had flown in from the New York office. She was delighted when Joe Bolker and his new wife, Victoria, joined her for a long weekend. She was thrilled when they told her that they had named their son, born earlier in the year, Alexander.

In spite of the unpromising beginning, the two weeks spent in California, with its appearance of a high-energy working vacation, satisfied Christina's need to be seen as something more serious than a 'rich, rich playgirl'. Between the talks with her Olympic managers, she swam in the Pacific for hours at a time. She preferred the ocean to either of the club's two heated pools. Basualdo ordered Clare to accompany the boss on her long dips. With not one ounce of fat to insulate her lithe body, little Clare would emerge from the water blue with cold, and teeth chattering. 'That's what we're being paid for,' he reminded her whenever she complained. Observing his unusual concept of *noblesse oblige*, Basualdo kept an eye on Christina from a beachside bar stool.

Summer on Skorpios on the surface began like all the other summers on the island. The Yturbes and the Doderos came; Henri and Atalanta de Castellane, Florence and brother Hubert, even the snarling Pongo, were there; Christina's schoolfriend Andrea de Montal brought Swiss interior designer Christophe Gollut; David d'Ambrumenil, now responsible for insuring the Onassis fleet, came with his fiancée Sarah Hodson. For his devotion to duty, Basualdo had been permitted to invite anyone he wished and he asked Christina's former stepsister Henrietta Spencer Churchill and her husband Nathan Gelber, 'Booby' to his friends. It was a mostly young crowd. Her father's friends, who had enjoyed the island's pleasures for so long, were uninvited now. 'It was not just that she wanted her own gang around her on Skorpios but that she wanted people who would perceive the island through her reality rather than Ari's ghost,' said one friend, who pointed out that there were no photographs of her father on view on Skorpios.

Those who were new to the scene were duly astonished by the luxury and style of the island. 'It's got everything but social workers and folk dancers,' remarked one English guest. Each villa had two maids exclusively assigned to it. Said first-time guest Christophe Gollut, 'You only have to drop your shirt on the floor for a second and it vanishes to come back perfectly laundered an hour later.' (An underground laundry worked around the clock in the season.) Guests too hungry to wait until 5 p.m. for lunch could nibble on crab, oysters, cold salmon, croissants, cheeses and cold cuts available at the delicatessen named Fauchon, after the Paris establishment whose famous delicacies it served. Further fresh food was imported daily from Athens; pastries and bread were made in Skorpios's own bakery. A chef was on duty twenty-four hours a day to prepare pizzas or grill steaks.

Guests tended to divide into national groups, with Basualdo (who this summer had been installed with little Clare in Christina's own marble pavilion) moving between them, ostensibly socializing, but in effect ensuring that no one monopolized or bored his employer – or, more important from his point of view, no man got too close to her. At lunch and dinner, Christina would invite two men to sit either side of her and there was always a courtly scramble for the remaining seats at her table. (Although eating with Christina was not such a joy, as Sarah Hodson pointed out: 'She's so *messy* . . . and talks with her mouth full.') In spite of some determined attempts to diet, Christina was fatter than at any time since she left Moscow. But she was not daunted by her size. She continued to wear her favourite Yves St Laurent skirts and blouses, although she knew they were designed for a much slimmer figure; when her thighs became too large for tights, she switched to knee stockings. Her proclivity for dancing continued to be extravagant and wearing on her guests: fuelled by her amphetamines, she would dance for hours after the nightly film show, Basualdo and little Clare taking it in turns to partner her when others fell from exhaustion.

But even surrounded by her own crowd, those she loved and trusted, and, she imagined, those who felt the same way about her, Christina never stayed relaxed or happy for very long. In such an internalized, cliquey community there were bound to be squabbles and petty jealousies, of course. Christina would start her day by giving Basualdo the names of those she was fed up with, citing some minor grievance or imagined slight (like a look she thought she had caught in somebody's face when she cut short a movie show); anyone who did not show sufficient enthusiasm for one of her suggestions automatically went into her bad books. Some who failed to observe the rules (no topless bathing, for example; no going to bed before she went to bed) were plucked off the island the same day.

Nobody was altogether safe from her wrath, and when Basualdo went on to her fed-up list because little Clare had been 'too possessive' over him – an unkind charge since Christina, pleading loneliness, often climbed into bed with them both, or beckoned Basualdo from Clare's sleeping arms to make love to her – he had a very precise idea of what to expect.

'You're not coming to Lefkas with us tomorrow,' Christina told him that evening. She knew he had been looking forward to that particular trip, which was to include his own special guests, Henrietta Spencer Churchill and Booby Gelber. 'Stay and take it easy with little Clare. I know she can't bear to be without you,' she said, her voice sweet with revenge.

He shrugged off his disappointment over not being allowed to accompany his friends on the trip. 'But sleeping with Clare that afternoon I had a premonition that something was going to go wrong. I always wanted to keep Christina to myself ... letting her loose in Lefkas wasn't a good idea,' he later recalled his recurring nightmare of being squeezed out of Christina's life by an unforeseen interloper.

At 9 p.m. when the party returned, his gravest apprehensions were realized. 'Madame has met a young man and invited him to dinner,' Eleni told him. 'He is still in his bathing costume, he needs to borrow a pair of trousers and a shirt.' Angry, disturbed, jealous, but also intensely curious, Basualdo followed Eleni to the villa where the visitor from Lefkas was waiting to be clothed. 'He was a Jewish boy, a Sephardic Jew, the son of a Tunisian rabbi from Marseilles, his name was Dovi Fitoussi,' Basualdo later recalled his first encounter with the small, skinny youth who stood in nothing but a pair of blue swimming briefs and a prayer-cap pinned to his hair. 'They met when she was about to return on the boat. He said, "Madame Christina, may I have a photograph taken with you, please?" Christina was flattered: Yes, yes, certainly. What's your name? Dovi? Hello, Dovi. What do you do? "I study medicine in Marseilles. I'm only nineteen and I would like a photograph with you." Would he like to come to Skorpios, and be photographed on her island? Of course he would, but he had no clothes. Don't worry, she said, we have lots of clothes on the island, and she loaded him on to the boat and brought him over.'

New guests had arrived, including British publisher Lord Weidenfeld and socialite Jean-Pierre Marcie-Rivière with his wife Rosemary. At dinner they were seated next to Christina. Dovi Fitoussi was put on a table with Basualdo and little Clare, who were under strict instructions to be nice to him. But he was ill at ease, and ate little of the rich fare. The movie that night was *Picnic at Hanging Rock*, which everyone enjoyed except Christina, who turned it off after an hour and called for the music to be put on and the dancing to begin. She asked Dovi to dance with her, which he did with as much style as anyone could expect from a man dancing in borrowed trousers cut several sizes too large for him. Nevertheless, it was clear that Christina was considerably taken with him and danced with other partners only out of sheer good manners.

At 4 a.m. Christina's thoughts began to drift away from music and dancing. 'She said to me, "Luis, Luis, I want that boy. But maybe he doesn't fancy me, maybe he doesn't find me attractive?" I guaranteed he would find her attractive, and went off to collect the little sonofabitch.' Basualdo found him deep in conversation with a pretty girl called Achille Foule, who seeing the look of mission on Basualdo's face quickly bid Dovi goodnight and slipped inside her villa. 'I said, "Listen, Dovi, Christina likes you very much and now we are going to her pavilion, do you understand?"' He hoped he had conveyed to the Tunisian son of a rabbi that 'Christina did not simply want to watch the sun come up with him.'

Stopping only to collect sustenance at Fauchon's (Dovi had eaten almost nothing at dinner), Basualdo took him to Christina's apartment. But Christina began to worry. 'I'm not sure that this is going to work, Luis. What shall I do if he doesn't get it together?' she asked Basualdo in English, a language Dovi apparently did not understand. 'I told her to check it out, sit close to him. If he got an erection, she was to say to me, "It was a nice day today, wasn't it, Luis?" and I would leave immediately. But she was still afraid that nothing would happen. I said, "Look, what's the worst thing that can happen? I get my pants back, get to beat the shit out of him and kick him off the island."'

Christina could not keep the sense of triumph out of her voice when a few minutes later she called to Basualdo, 'Luis, wasn't it a nice day today?'

'At 8.15, not even two hours later, she came bursting into my bedroom shouting, "Luis, Luis, you thought I was too fat, you are crazy! He did it three times, *three times*!" I said, "Good for you, Christina," but she said, "No, no, you are upset, Luis, you are angry. You want to dominate me, you want to control me and not let another man get near me." I said, "Of course not. I want your happiness. I'm glad that it has worked out with Dovi."'

He knew it was a psychological as well as a sexual triumph for Christina, and that she would attach a disproportionate importance to Dovi Fitoussi in her life. Meanwhile, there were only four more days left of the holiday on Skorpios and she did not want to waste a minute. The helicopter was despatched to collect Dovi's clothes, although he was barely seen outside her pavilion for the rest of the stay. When it was time to part, she gave him her private number in St Moritz, and asked him to call her as soon as he got home. 'But it's very expensive to call Switzerland from Marseilles. My father won't permit it,' he said. She gave him $10,000. 'Call me,' she said, as he boarded the helicopter that would take him to Actium, where her Learjet waited to fly him home to Marseilles.

Back at the Villa Cristal, Christina waited for Dovi Fitoussi's calls with the kind of pleasurable anxiety with which she had not long ago waited for Nicky Mavroleon's calls. But Dovi did not let her down. The first day he called and spoke with her for over an hour. The following day he called and talked to her for another hour. On the third day he called – collect! 'Ten thousand dollars for two phone calls – I don't think even Christina Onassis can afford this fellow,' Basualdo told her gleefully, convinced that this was the end of the affair. 'Now you can forget about him,' he said. 'But she said, "Luis, you don't want me to have a boyfriend, you want me all to yourself. You want to dominate me, control me, take all my money."' Money was a consideration, if not at the heart of their relationship, Luis Basualdo conceded that, but he also wanted her to be happy. 'And this boy would never make her happy. It could never have worked. His age, religion, background – it was out of the question.'

Meanwhile, Christina was still pursuing her 'black beauties' regime of two days on, one day clean, and as always on the third day she craved activity to take her mind off things; trips to Venice continued to be a favourite distraction. Returning to the airport one evening, they were told that they would not get back to Samaden before the control tower closed for the day. 'Where can we go?' she asked Luis, quickly supplying the answer: 'I know, let's go to Marseilles.' It was the worst news that Basualdo and Clare could hear, but she would not be dissuaded.

They booked into the Sofitel Marignon, a modern airport hotel several grades below that to which Christina was accustomed. 'She called a taxi, we didn't have a car in Marseilles, and told the driver to take us to Le Cannet, but the driver said, "Oh, Madame, we don't go there at night, it's very dangerous." She wouldn't be put off. I left her at the house. She said she wanted to be alone with the family. She ate couscous or whatever, and stayed until four in the morning. Finally, she convinced Dovi to return to the Sofitel,' Basualdo recalled the adventure in Marseilles.

The following morning Christina confessed that Dovi was no longer the man he had been on Skorpios. 'His father, the rabbi, had told him he mustn't sleep with her as they weren't getting married. So Dovi obediently slept between the sheets and insisted that Christina sleep on top. She was so cold she had to send for a duvet,' Basualdo said.

Christina's disappointment was especially keen since she had shown the utmost goodwill towards the whole Fitoussi family, offering to ship all thirteen of them to Paris with Dovi, who was 'le soleil de la maison', according to the rabbi. 'My organization will arrange everything. You will all have jobs. I promise,' she said. For two days Dovi and Christina did not leave her suite at the Sofitel while she harried her office to organize the mass transfer, and pleaded personally with the Minister of Education to arrange a place in a Paris medical school for Dovi, who was still not letting her near his body.

Basualdo knew that several of his English friends were over in St Tropez and he suggested it might break the tension at the Sofitel if they drove over for a day. Christina preferred to persevere with Dovi but invited Luis to take little Clare off for the day.

Christina's problems, which had so upset his enjoyment of life, seemed far removed as Luis sunbathed and lunched at Cinquante Cinq, the most fashionable meeting place on Pampelonne beach, where they met up with baronet Sir William Pigott-Brown, a former amateur champion jockey, and legendary London lounge lizard Rupert Deen, and their group. After dinner in the port of St Tropez, Basualdo regretfully started the journey back to the Sofitel and the continuing drama of Dovi Fitoussi. At reception he was handed an envelope. Inside was a note from Christina and a wad of French banknotes. 'I have returned to Paris. Here's money for your flight. *C'est le fin de Dovi,*' she had written.

After four sexless nights, Christina had called it a day.

—12—

Love lasteth as long as the money endureth

William Caxton
The Game of Chesse

CHRISTINA HAD ALWAYS APPRECIATED whatever advantages her mother's marriage to Sunny Blandford brought her. And although she had evolved her own culture – she was and ever would be an Onassis, and Greek – she felt an affinity with Sunbun and his English aristocratic family. She counted her childhood years at Lee Place among the happiest of her life. Memories of those halcyon times 'a lifetime ago' must have been in her mind when the duke called her in Paris early one Sunday morning shortly after the Dovi Fitoussi affair and told her that her former stepbrother, James, the Marquess of Blandford, was in serious trouble.

He had become a heroin addict. Moreover, he had discharged himself from a drug rehabilitation clinic in Minnesota, and his future seemed bleak. To the distress of a disappointed father, Sunny added an inherited anxiety about the family fortune. To avoid crippling death duties, Blenheim Palace had already been made over to James. Should he die early, as heroin addicts are prone to do, the family would be exposed to massive demands under a capital transfer tax. It would almost certainly mean the end of the great estate, and perhaps the beginning of the end of a great English family.

Although he did not come into his inheritance for another four years, when he would be thirty, James in the meantime was buying all the dope he needed on credit. Since he and James had drifted a little bit out of sympathy with one another, the duke asked Christina to help. Christina knew that these confessions cost Sunbun an effort and she promised to do everything she could to save her former stepbrother. The duke's request was given an added resonance because of its timing: for despite her satisfaction at having extricated herself from the Fitoussi fiasco, she had been feeling at a loss, and a little detached from things since her return to Paris. 'It's always easier to look after someone else than after oneself,' she remarked when she told Basualdo the story. Although she had seen little of James since their childhood, when they had been extremely fond of each other, Christina promised Sunbun that she would find him (he was on the loose in London), and persuade him to stay with her at the Villa Cristal, where she planned to keep him away from the pushers and 'talk some sense into him'.

It took time to track him down and Christina's own addiction to amphetamines was as insidious as ever when, early in the New Year, he pitched up at the Villa Cristal with his girlfriend Lulu Blacker. 'Christina had completely changed, she was a nightmare,' James later remembered the visit. 'She had to be entertained all day, all night. She was on a diet so no one else was allowed to eat, no one was allowed to get close to food, the servants saw to it! She could not sit still. We'd watch a video and half-way through – click! – just in the good part, she'd say, "Let's go to King's." Then just as we were enjoying ourselves at King's, she'd want to go back and watch the rest of the video. Then it was back again to King's or the Dracula, five or six in the morning, just because of the pills. She was fat, her teeth were green, but nothing that a good tooth-brush wouldn't sort out. She never actually smelled, because Eleni wouldn't let her smell, she was simply yucky. I never enjoyed St Moritz. I had bad experiences there.'

It was during this visit that Christina tumbled into love again. The new object of her haphazard passion was David Davies, a tall, amusing Englishman whose good looks had won him at Oxford the nickname Beauty. Davies had been best man at his cousin David d'Ambrumenil's marriage to Sarah Hodson, and, following the reception at the Savoy Hotel in London, was among the dozen guests (including the Marlboroughs) who accompanied the bride and groom to St Moritz in George Livanos's jet. At a dinner party at the Chesa Veglia the following evening, Christina was placed next to Davies, whom she had never met before. He was forty-two, divorced (from New York banking heiress Debbie Loeb) and the finance director of Britain's second largest property company. He was also a natural flirt, and over the caviar-covered pizzas Christina enjoyed his full attention. He too was impressed with the fact that she did not disguise her interest in him ('obviously she fancied him rotten,' the bride Sarah d'Ambrumenil said flatly), even though his steady girlfriend Phyllida Fellowes was sitting opposite, alongside the watchful Luis Basualdo. And she was quick off the mark when Davies casually let drop that he would shortly be in Paris on business. 'Call me,' she said. 'Maybe we can have some dinner. Your cousin has my numbers.'

It is unlikely that Phyllida, whose marriage to Lord de Ramsey's son and heir John Fellowes was heading for divorce, was unduly apprehensive when she returned to London the next day while Davies headed for Paris. On the face of it, Christina offered no competition at all. She was fat (she had actually contrived to *put on* sixteen pounds in seven days in a Swiss health hydro) and 'about as sexy,' in Basualdo's cruel phrase, 'as a wallowing hippo'. But Phyllida did not reckon with the allure of a fabulous fortune, which makes nonsense of beauty and statistics. Certainly Christina was not surprised when Davies called and arranged to take her to dinner at a small discreet restaurant away from the prying lenses of the paparazzi.

She was thrilled with what she euphemistically called her conquest. When she later described in detail to Basualdo her night with Davies ('the first time was not so good, the next morning was fantastic') he recognized the advent of another disastrous affair with its inevitable knock-on effect on his own happiness and well-being. 'Don't go on with this,' he pleaded with her. 'This man has a terrible reputation with women. He will only hurt you.' Not only would she not listen to him but she went ahead and arranged a meeting with Davies in Aspen, where he was joining David and Sarah d'Ambrumenil, who were continuing their honeymoon in the Colorado ski resort.

Basualdo did what he could to end the affair quickly, airing plans that Davies would have preferred to remain private.

'The next thing we know Basualdo is ringing us up and saying, "Oh your cousin" et cetera, because Christina had told him David had done it, this was three days after the dinner party in St Moritz,' recalls Sarah d'Ambrumenil. 'My David was very cross with David Davies. He said, "You're so stupid, you're doing it for just another notch."'

The Aspen assignation got off to a bad start and went downhill. They met at Colorado's Stapleton International Airport and caught an Air Aspen flight to the resort. Snow flurries were coming in from the Rockies when they took off, and conditions worsened so rapidly that the flight had to be diverted to Grand Junction, from where they were to be coached to Aspen. It was only when they were on the coach, and, according to Sarah d'Ambrumenil, Christina 'appeared to know all the other people on the bus', that Davies realized that she was not alone. Although in fact she had limited her entourage to three (her nurse Veronique, a woman to look after her hair and makeup, and Eleni), Davies was not pleased. He had arranged to stay with a Canadian friend, David Gilmore, and his English wife Jill, and he knew that their apartment in the Aspen Club was not large enough to accommodate the extra staff.

The Greyhound bus ride from Grand Junction to Aspen took nearly five hours in appalling conditions, and an exhausted, jet-lagged Christina collapsed alone into bed after a late supper with their hosts. Davies went on to a party. And when she woke up the following morning, he had already left to go skiing (with an exceptionally pretty guide, she discovered later). She arranged to ski with Sarah, who had also lost her David for the day 'and was in a pretty foul mood'. But Sarah was surprised by Christina's look of utter dejection and disappointment.

'It was snowing, not nice weather, and she came and sat next to me on the fence at the bottom of Aspen mountain. She used to call me "Pigletino", and she said, "Pigletino, I really don't like it here. It's not like St Moritz." Meaning, I suppose, that she wasn't in control,' Sarah remembers. Aspen was a glamorous town in its most glamorous season: the men's World Cup skiing championships were in full swing, and celebrity residents like Jack Nicholson, Jill St John and John Denver gave it the showbiz pizzazz that Christina enjoyed. But she just couldn't get into the swing of it. She was invited to dinner that evening by Bob Hefner, an oil and gas magnate and the d'Ambrumenils' host in Aspen, but she never arrived.

'The next thing we knew she'd gone,' says Sarah, who suspects that the town 'wasn't what she expected at all . . . and she didn't have David's undivided attention.' (Far from it: Davies had confessed to Sarah that 'he couldn't make love to her at all' in Aspen.)

But the handsome Englishman's failure to perform in Aspen (which Christina optimistically ascribed to the malign influences of altitude and cold weather rather than any serious lack of interest on his part) served only to increase her infatuation. Like so many men before him, Davies had suddenly and unknowingly become the light and air of her life. For weeks she tried to reach him on his London number without success, and became mysteriously convinced that he was somehow refusing to answer only her calls. 'I know he's there,' she told Basualdo.

Finally, she flew to London and knocked on Davies's door, which was opened by Sarah d'Ambrumenil. Sarah had just moved into the apartment while her husband's new Chelsea house was being decorated. She explained that Davies was in Ireland, visiting his father's estate in County Wicklow. 'We talked and she said she was still in love with him and wanted to get back with him. "Pigletino, can you help?" she said.'

The *amourette* had been an embarrassment to David d'Ambrumenil, who worried that his own business relationship, as well as his long friendship, with Christina could be jeopardized by his cousin's inconsiderate toying. He called Davies in Ireland and told him to at least meet with Christina and level with her face to face. Davies flew to London and let the heiress down as gently as he could. She returned to Paris and said to Basualdo, 'You were right and I was wrong. How could I have been so foolish? Even Vivien Clore called to warn me that he was bad news. I should have listened to you both, Luis.'

But encouraged by this new avowal of dependency on his good judgement and shrewd advice, Luis Basualdo became a little too confident about his place in her affections. Christina knew all about his little scams and weaknesses, which had earned him the epithet 'the bounder' among her friends and in the British press. She turned a blind eye to the fact that even though she gave him $250 a day to take Clare to lunch, Eleni complained that they always returned at three and raided the icebox! She even went along with the $500 a day he charged to bring the concierge's cat up to the fifth floor to keep her cocker spaniel Yuri company. (Basualdo, who saw this as one of the legitimate perks that almost doubled his $1,000-a-day salary, recalls the bargaining session that fixed the cat fee: 'She said, "Luis, Luis, go get Madame Magy's cat so little Yuri has a friend to play with." I am terrified of cats and I know that this cat is a very wild animal. I told her this and she said, "I will give you one hundred dollars." No way, I said. "Two hundred." No way. "Three hundred." I still say no, and she said, "I will give you five hundred." I said, okay, pay me up front. But she said she would pay me when I delivered the cat. So I ring Madame Magy's doorbell and she's out and there's her little daughter there. I say, "Hello, little girl.

Can I borrow your cat for a little while?" "No, no," she cried. "The cat never leaves *la maison*, never." "Oh, come on, little girl, I need that cat now," and I put a fifty-franc piece in her mouth and grab the cat. So I was making $500 a day just bringing the cat to play with Yuri. But one day the stupid cat scratched Yuri and that was the end.')

Nevertheless, even understanding Basualdo's keen interest in finding new ways of making money, she did not hesitate to give him £3,000 to pass on to Rodney Solomon, an old friend who was temporarily down on his luck. Basualdo informed Solomon that Christina wanted to give him £1,000 – but he would have to sign a receipt for £3,000! Solomon obliged, but later mentioned the unusual condition to David d'Ambrumenil. D'Ambrumenil immediately told Christina, and Luis Basualdo was at last told to leave Avenue Foch.

Yet, astonishingly, he remained on the payroll. 'I will always look after you, Luis,' she told him with the sentimental loyalty that was always a weakness with her. To settle his nerves, and to make up for his disappointment at losing Avenue Foch and all its wondrous perks, she promised that only when another man came into her life would she let him go – with a million-dollar kiss-off. It seemed an eminently fair arrangement to Basualdo, and it was an arrangement he was not likely to forget.

It was not the best of times for Christina. The news that Nicky Mavroleon had married Nicaraguan beauty Barbara Carrera, an actress who had appeared with Sean Connery in the latest James Bond movie *Never Say Never Again*, opened the old wound for a week or two. And her relationship with the Greek government continued to be stormy and ambivalent. A month after president Constantine Karamanlis presented the Alexander Onassis Foundation Awards ($100,000 each to Polish film maker Andrzej Wajda, Lord Duncan-Sandys and Prince Sadruddin Aga Khan), which it was hoped would create a philanthropic image for the Onassis name in Greece, an Athens court ruled that she must pay $32.5 million in death duties, and fines for failing to submit tax declarations. Stelios Papadimitriou continued to argue that Ari had been a citizen of Argentina and the real estate, including Skorpios and two villas at Glyfada, was controlled by foreign companies not liable to Greek tax.

Her weight soaring above 180 pounds, in July Christina again turned to Sergei Kauzov (who had proclaimed his Russian fondness for large women) for companionship and understanding. Ignoring their last bad experience in California, they returned to La Jolla for several weeks of such conspicuous togetherness that rumours of remarriage became rife.

They were still only rumours when she returned to Paris via London, where she briefly visited her $1.5 million apartment on Eaton Square, and met Sunbun, the Duke of Marlborough, to discuss the continuing problem of James Blandford. She recognized that James's stay with her in St Moritz had not been an all-round success, she said. But now she had discovered a very fine drug clinic called Château Gage, a formidable fortress of a place on the outskirts of Paris, and suggested a plan to get the young heir committed. Sunbun was grateful for any help he could get at this stage of his son's addiction, and encouraged her to go ahead.

James was living in the basement flat of American art dealer Billy Keating's house in Tite Street, Chelsea. Christina called Keating and told him her plan. He was to bring the marquess to Paris, ostensibly for a weekend at Avenue Foch. She would send her Learjet to pick them up at noon on Friday at Luton airport.

James smiled to himself as he sank into the deep soft leather armchairs of the Lear. He smiled when 'four monkeys in white coats' told him he had to be strapped on to a stretcher so they could switch on the siren to cut through the traffic. He smiled because he had just done several lines of cocaine. 'I thought, this is a novel way of getting to Avenue Foch,' he later recalled the journey. 'But we didn't go anywhere near Avenue Foch. Twenty minutes later we are outside these enormous gates. Château Gage. I was a bit hot under the collar at this stage. I thought, bloody hell, this is a major conspiracy, this is.'

He sobered up fast. Locked in a bare room, he took stock of the situation. 'This is bad news, I think to myself. This is a perishing nuthouse. I've got to get out of here.' He asked for a cup of coffee with sugar, praying that they would bring a spoon. They did. Left alone, he used the spoon to unscrew the window, climbed out and dropped twenty feet to the ground. 'I leaped across this bloody big garden, shinned up a rusty old ladder attached to a water-tower contraption and swung over the wall.'

His luck was in. On the other side of the wall was an unattended bread-delivery scooterette, its engine running. 'I jumped on it and kept going till I came to a Metro station. I stopped a man and said, "You are not going to believe this, but my stepsister has kidnapped me and tried to put me in Château Gage." His face fell a mile. I said, "All I want is twenty francs to get to Paris." He gave me a hundred-franc note. I said, "You really are too kind." Anyway, I got into the middle of Paris and got to the *gare* which goes out to Charles de Gaulle. Fortunately, I still had my Diners Club card in my jeans and managed to get a seat on the last plane back to London. I had to get back because I had had some smack that morning and was beginning to withdraw ...'

A few minutes after James arrived back at Tite Street, Billy Keating returned. Unbeknownst to each other, they had been on the same flight. James did not blame him for his abduction beyond pointing out that it was not of a kind that helped drug addicts towards recovery. Instead, he called Christina. 'I went mad and called her every single name I could think of. She was ghastly, disloyal ... I never want to see you again, sort of thing. I then did the same to my father who was at Lee Place, and that was that. Things calmed down. They realized it was a nasty thing to have done. It was just the most terrible shock. "Houdini Blandford" was the headline in the *Daily Mail*.'

The episode was a great disappointment to Christina and spoiled the start of her shortened low-key summer on Skorpios (she felt it would be unwise to be too conspicuous while pursuing her tax wrangle with the Greek government), which ended badly too. On Sunday, 28 August, she was held for three hours for questioning by customs officials at the Actium military airstrip before being allowed to leave the country in her Learjet. It was clear to her that the affront at Actium, where her father had enjoyed landing privileges and virtual diplomatic immunity for twenty years, was a warning that the Onassis name had lost its power in Athens. 'I think the game is up,' she told a friend in Paris shortly before she finally settled with the Greeks for a modest $3.7 million – after threatening to suspend work on a model heart hospital the Foundation was building in Athens.

The frequency of her divorces and affairs strengthened Christina's conviction that she would never be happily in love for very long. But in 1983, a few days after her thirty-third birthday, something happened that gave her new hope. In the foyer of Claridge's in London she bumped into Henri Roussel. Henri, who had a practised but frequently engaging charm, and adored intrigue as much as he disapproved of his son's longtime mistress Gaby Landhage, lost no time in assuring Christina that Thierry talked of her frequently and always with great warmth. 'I know he would love to see you again,' he told her.

Encouraged by the accidental meeting with Henri Roussel, and with rekindled memories of her seduction on Skorpios ten years before, Christina asked Florence Grinda to find Thierry's number in Kenya for her. 'I want to wish him a happy Christmas,' she explained, nonchalantly passing over the decade that had elapsed since last they met, or even spoke together.

If Thierry was surprised to get her call he did not show it. They told each other what had happened in their lives. His long affair with Gaby was over. She had made a name for herself as a nude model for photographer Gunnar Larsen before returning to Sweden, where she now worked as an executive with a cosmetics company. He had fallen in love with another Scandinavian fashion model, Kirsten Gille, but that affair too had ended. He dabbled in business in France and Algeria. He had a majority interest in a Paris model agency called First, which he was planning to sell to a Swiss consortium. He spent up to five months a year at Oljogi (Swahili for 'Place of Many Thorns'), the family's 50,000-acre estate in Kenya. He made his life sound both idyllic and strangely celibate.

Christina could not believe her luck. 'He's totally unattached. He spends most of his day fishing for rainbow trout and waiting for my calls,' she told a Paris friend. She had not felt a physical attraction as powerful as this since Nicky Mavroleon. She couldn't think about anything else. They talked to each other every day, and when the conversation eventually veered towards the possibility of a meeting, she confessed that she had put on some weight since 1973. 'I don't want you to see me like this,' she told him. Thierry told her to go to a health clinic in Marbella, the Buschinger, which the top Paris models used and swore by. 'Lose eighty pounds and I'll marry you,' he told her imperiously.

She took him half-seriously and flew the next day to Marbella and booked into the clinic for an indefinite stay. Thierry sent flowers every day, with encouraging messages. The days dragged, but the weight began to fall away. She whiled away the hours calling everyone she knew, including Luis Basualdo, who was staying in Sir Gordon White's villa above the Palace Hotel in Gstaad. One day she rang and he said he had a surprise for her: Danny Marentette came on the line. 'Hello, Danny,' she said in an exaggerated drawl, speaking to her very first lover for the first time in almost fourteen years. 'How are you doing, financially?' It was a question she liked to ask old friends. 'Well,' he told her, laying it on a bit thick, 'I'm broke and have been all my life, and as I get older it's less appealing, but I'm living with it. How are you doing, financially?' 'Not one of my problems,' Christina said.

She hadn't lost eighty pounds when she returned to Paris and Thierry at the beginning of February, but she had lost enough to look better than she had looked for a very long time. She felt wonderful. Her slimmed-down face had recaptured its look of strength and striking sensuality. Her teeth were polished, her thick black hair shone with health. It was as if the years since they last met had never happened, and as if Buschinger had emptied her of all the turmoil and sadness she had locked inside herself. They moved into Avenue Foch together with an alacrity that alarmed many of her friends, but surprised nobody who knew her well. 'I want to marry and have children, what do you want?' she asked him. 'Exactly the same,' he told her.

—13—

A love without indiscretion is no love at all

Thomas Hardy
The Hand of Ethelberta

AND SO, THREE WEEKS AFTER THEIR ENGAGEMENT, announced at
a party at the Paris discothèque Palace on 23 February 1984, the man
Christina had first met as a schoolboy at Florence Grinda's wedding,
the Apollo-like youth she had made love to on Skorpios ten years before,
the golden boy who had won even her father's approval, at last became
her fourth husband. 'People say the marriage is too sudden,' she had
told a girlfriend as she steamed and starved herself to shed another
twenty pounds at the Marbella clinic in order to fit into her $10,000
Christian Dior cream silk wedding dress. 'It isn't sudden at all. I've
waited ten years for this man. I don't intend to let him get away a second
time.'

As if to be sure, Christina insisted on marrying him twice: a civil
ceremony at the Paris sixteenth *arrondissement* town hall on 17 March
was immediately followed by a romantic candlelit service at a Greek
Orthodox church. Jean-Noël Grinda was best man, and the three
Livanos sisters, Arietta, Eugenie and Marina, were bridesmaids. In the
evening there was a dinner for 150 guests at Maxim's. Friends travelled
from New York and London, from Athens and Los Angeles and Rome
to be there.

Christina must have felt a supreme sense of triumph and control as
she told guests over and over again, 'I am just very, very happy. We are
wonderfully in love,' and heard her groom telling the same story, adding:
'We want to have children and grow old together.' But it was the
rumoured abundance of Christina's wedding gifts to her husband that
created the excitement and caused the tongues to wag. As dinner pro-

141

gressed from the caviar and iced Russian vodka to bisque of terrapin, seafood in pastry with truffles, and through the racks of lamb and chocolate soufflés, and Christina continued to declare her happiness, and receive the felicitations, the whisper that she had given Thierry $10 million went from table to table, followed by the even more spectacular story that he had not even been asked to sign a marriage contract; an oversight which, if they were to separate, would entitle him to 50 per cent of the community property.

Certainly his bride's largesse could not have come at a more propitious time for Thierry. His agency First was losing money, and there was talk that a major Algerian deal had gone spectacularly amiss, and he had been anxiously trying to raise new finance. But if Christina knew any of this that night at Maxim's it did not show, and perhaps she did not care. 'I'm a changed woman,' she told Adnan Khashoggi, one of several billionaires among the wedding guests (and one of the reasons why Christina thought it prudent to hire twenty-five bodyguards to keep an eye on the party). 'I've had ten terrible years since my father's death. Thierry has given back to me faith in myself,' she said.

After the honeymoon in the West Indies they returned to Avenue Foch (where Sergei Kauzov had thoughtfully left a Mercedes 450SEL in the garage as a wedding present to his ex-wife) and started looking for a house in Paris. Meanwhile, Thierry insisted on keeping his own apartment in the rue de la Tour Maubourg, near Les Invalides, professing to be uncomfortable in the Onassis apartment which he found 'too old'.

According to Luis Basualdo, at this time Christina had $330 million in time deposits from which she was collecting a tax-free income of nearly a million dollars a week. But her annual expenses were no more than $6 million. Few human weaknesses are so quickly aroused as vanity in those who are the favourites of fortune, and it was not long before Thierry, aware of the unspent millions almost at his fingertips, was suggesting some improvements in their lifestyle. Her Learjet, he said, was uncomfortable; it didn't even have a toilet (an omission that had been critically noted by James Blandford on his journey to France). Why not buy something larger, a transatlantic model? He drew her attention to the virtues of the three-engined Falcon 50. It had a range of 3,450 miles, cruised at 500 miles an hour, and cost only $15 million. Proud of being Mrs Roussel, the name by which she now wanted to be known, still dazzled by her husband's attentive ways, and impressed for some reason by his business acumen ('friends tried to correct her ideas in this respect, but in vain,' said one Paris friend who failed), Christina ordered a ten-seater model, fitted with bedroom and bathroom, and painted white with red and blue chevrons. Similarly encouraged to upgrade her London residence, she acquired a $1.3 million four-bedroom apartment in Grosvenor Square, close to the block where George Livanos and the Niarchos brothers owned flats.

At the beginning of July, Thierry chartered Baron Heini Thyssen's yacht, the *Hansa*, and with ten friends set out for Skorpios, via the Mediterranean and the annual summer party Houston hostess Lynn Wyatt gave at La Mauresque, Somerset Maugham's former home on St Jean-Cap Ferrat. Christina had never been happier. Not only was she with the man she loved but she was also expecting his child. On Skorpios her friends found her 'blissful', allowing Thierry to run the place, a privilege never permitted to any of her other husbands or lovers. Christina's English set had been replaced by Thierry's French friends, probably because he spoke very little English and resented it when Christina conversed in her preferred and most comfortable language.

The day she learned she was pregnant Christina put herself in cotton wool. She quit her amphetamine regime 'cold turkey'. It was not going to be an easy pregnancy, she told friends: 'I can't take any risks.' Florence Grinda says, 'She could barely move. She had to stay in bed a lot.' She gave up all pretence of running her company. 'I have delegated most of my Olympic responsibilities to my father's team. I want to concentrate on my wifely business,' she said. But she still ran her family like a subsidiary of some international business conglomerate, which, in a sense, it was. In order to establish Swiss residency for inheritance purposes, she took a permanent suite in Le Richemond Hotel in Geneva while they searched for a suitable home in Switzerland in which to bring up a family.

Superstitiously refusing a scan, Christina was convinced she was carrying a daughter. Still secretly in touch with Basualdo (Thierry deeply disapproved of the Argentinian and forbade Christina even to mention Basualdo's name in his presence), Christina called him almost daily in London and talked about her plans, and occasionally asked him to do things for her, perhaps to make her feel she was getting something for the money she continued to pay him. Her daughter would be born in Paris, she told him; she had already chosen her name, Athina, and engaged the French gynaecologist Professor Michel Lanvin, to whom, she said, she was paying 'a million dollars for a safe delivery'. She had booked five rooms at the American Hospital for the last week in January.

She celebrated her thirty-fourth birthday in Geneva; her new Falcon 50 collected ten friends from Paris for a dinner party in Le Gentilhomme Grill at Le Richemond. ('Private jetliners are nothing special now, but Christina is the only person in the world I know who keeps hers completely exclusive. She could help cover its costs if she rented it out occasionally, but she refuses: the plane, the pilots, the mechanics – they wait,' said Patrice Habans, a French photographer who had known her since she was a child.)

To relieve the monotony of her own 'dull, tranquil, tedious condition', Christina insisted on being told everything that was happening in her old haunts and in the lives of her favourite people. Philippe Niarchos told her that his girlfriend, Victoria Guinness, was also expecting a child in the spring and that his father, notwithstanding his own personal proclivities in these matters, was 'not terribly pleased'.

The reason for Stavros's displeasure was not that Philippe and Victoria were to become unmarried parents and he a natural grandfather, but that Victoria's late father, Patrick, was the Aga Khan's half-brother – and Stavros was not at that moment speaking to the spiritual leader of twelve million Ismaili Muslims. The feud began in July when the Aga Khan, familiarly known as K, spent a week on Spetsopoula with his wife Sally, his daughter Princess Zahra, and sons Prince Rahim and Prince Hussain. Also on the island was Stavros's son Spyros, and the girl he hoped to marry, Pilar Goess. Miss Goess, who had appeared nude in a 1977 German edition of *Playboy* magazine, and was in every way a remarkable Austrian beauty, was greatly admired by K. When he sailed away aboard his yacht *Amaloun*, Miss Goess's heart sailed with him. She told Spyros that their four-year relationship was over.

Christina urged her cousins to 'do something . . . the honour of your family is at stake.' But only Constantine, perhaps because he was genuinely fond of her, perhaps because he wanted to show his appreciation for the occasional $15,000 she slipped him when his dope habit (he had been expelled from Harrow for smoking pot) got him into financial scrapes, only Constantine took her at her word.

While Christina continued to rest quietly at Villa Cristal, her confinement less than five weeks away, Constantine sent a frisson of scandal and shock through St Moritz. After celebrating Christmas Eve at the King's Club, he managed to gain access to the Aga Khan's suite at the Chesa Garda Ley Hotel and confront 'the spiritual leader of twelve million – and a one-off *Playboy* nude' (to whom K reputedly had given a most incarnate $2 million pink diamond) with a shower of coins: 'You love money so much, here's some more of it,' he shouted into K's astonished, sleep-filled face.

'Bravo, Tino,' Christina told him when she heard the story later that Christmas morning.

On 29 January 1985, at the American Hospital in Paris where Aristotle Socrates Onassis had died a decade before, Christina gave birth by Caesarean section to a six-pound two-ounce girl named Athina, after her grandmother. (As in so many things in Christina's life, confusion and rumour surrounded the birth of her baby, and deepened further when the infant was moved to the Necker Hospital, where there were intensive care facilities for premature babies. 'Reports that the baby is ill are a tissue of lies,' said Professor Lanvin. 'Mother and baby are in perfect health.' But paediatrician Dr Michel Demont did nothing to clear up the mystery when he told the press, 'Imagine that we have an engine which we must start. As time goes by, it starts ticking over and then bursts into life. For this it is essential for the baby to avoid any infections affecting heart, lungs or digestive organs. So she has been moved to Necker, which is perhaps the best in Europe for children. The world's greatest specialists have been called in.')

Whatever the reality of the early dramas of Athina's life, by April she had grown into a healthy and rather pretty little baby, watched over night and day by two nannies and an armed bodyguard. Christina had called off her search for a new home in Paris when she acquired the flat above her first-floor apartment on Avenue Foch and created a duplex (decorated by Atalanta de Castellane) for her and Thierry, keeping the fifth floor for entertaining. Under Thierry's direction, the household had more than doubled and now included two chefs (François, who had worked for the Shah of Iran, and Christian, his under-chef); two chauffeurs (his and hers): Hélène, the chief housekeeper; Yves Terrier, head waiter; two maids (Maria, a Spaniard, and Francine, who was French); the nursery staff; and Eleni and her husband George, who had retired as chauffeur after an accident, but continued to make himself useful around the house and on Skorpios. In addition to Avenue Foch there was now a $2.3 million, eighteen-room 'family house' called Boislande, set in lakeside parkland at Gingins, twelve miles outside Geneva, with a staff of ten; a married couple ran Villa Cristal; forty people were employed full-time on Skorpios. The Paris staff was transferred at weekends to the Roussel estate at Sologne ('too cold and too miserable-looking,' complained Christina, who hated the weekend upheaval and soon put a stop to it) to augment its small team of cook, gamekeeper, and gardener. The Falcon had two pilots and a steward, with another pilot for the Italian Augusta helicopter.

A very good insight into the Onassis–Roussel household at this time comes from Yves Terrier, who was taken on a month after the birth of Athina. Lunching with the rest of the staff on his first day at Avenue Foch he was surprised to be offered caviar, lobster and Dom Perignon 1981, one of the finest vintages of one of the world's finest champagnes. 'Madame says everybody who works for her should be happy,' Hélène explained the commendable staff menu. 'She insists that what she eats the servants eat. There was a dinner party on the fifth floor last night for fifty people. We will be eating caviar and lobster for days, I'm afraid.'

Privately Christina preferred plainer food. She usually lunched alone; most days she asked for a rare steak, with a green salad, which she ate with her fingers. This startled Yves Terrier, as did her first order: 'Fetch me a Diet Coke.' The drink was not available in France; each week Christina's ten-seater jet was despatched to New York to bring back precisely one hundred bottles. 'Why not a thousand bottles?' Yves asked Hélène. 'Because Madame doesn't want *old* Diet Coke,' Hélène explained, and suggested that he serve it with considerable respect since it worked out at $300 a bottle. Thierry joined his wife for dinner, which, because Christina was usually on a diet, tended to be soup, chicken and salad. Thierry, who drank very little, would sip a glass of white Burgundy, while his wife often got through over a thousand dollars' worth of Diet Coke. Her thirst for what she called 'my one-calorie tipple' never ceased to surprise the staff at Avenue Foch: at 7 a.m. one morning she walked into the kitchen and, ignoring Terrier having his breakfast, collected several bottles from the fridge to take back to her bedroom. Beneath the short T-shirt, as she leaned over into the fridge, Yves Terrier could not fail to see that she was 'bare-assed naked'.

The waiter's surprise at his mistress's *deshabille* was only exceeded by his astonishment that she was doing something for herself – if she dropped her spectacles she would wait for them to be picked up; when her Walkman wires became entangled, she would call a servant to untangle them. ('Her autocratic attitude didn't stop at servants. She found people in every class who were willing to serve her in some way,' said one Skorpios regular.) Few days passed at Avenue Foch in which the new member of staff did not encounter some new impressive detail – from Christina's seven-foot by five-foot rose marble bathtub ('Madame likes to bathe with her husband,' explained Hélène) to a permanently dust-sheeted BMW520 car in the garage (hired for a guest who never arrived, the car had remained there: every month a hire bill was presented and paid).

The rich buy houses to conceal their whereabouts, and between Boislande and Avenue Foch and the Villa Cristal, between Skorpios and Sologne, and Thierry's place on rue de la Tour Maubourg, and Christina's Eaton Square apartment in London (she had changed her mind about the Grosvenor Square flat and sold it even before she had moved in, taking a £45,000 profit), it was hardly noticed that Mr and Mrs Roussel did not spend a great deal of time together. 'Thierry comes and goes. Sometimes I do not see him for a week, and that is good for the marriage,' Christina told Florence Grinda, who with typical French cynicism in matters marital 'thought it was very nice for Thierry too'.

Whether Florence already knew something Christina didn't know she will not say, but she was apprehensive about Christina's tendency to yell and scream whenever she had a bone to pick with Thierry. 'The trouble with you Greeks,' she warned her friend, 'is that you rave and scream too much. Thierry is a Frenchman. You can't win an argument with a Frenchman if you rant and scream at him.'

But Christina soon had good reason to scream, and loudly. Within weeks of marrying Christina, Thierry had started seeing Gaby Landhage again. And now the beautiful Swede was pregnant. 'She heard about Gaby and the baby at a dinner party, I don't know whose,' says Florence. 'I said I would never stand for that. The poor girl was utterly distraught. She said she was going to get a divorce.'

Ordered out of Boislande, Roussel took a suite at the Hôtel Beau Rivage, in Geneva. He was convinced that her tantrum ('I give you everything, money, a child, and now you humiliate me. You've had the last penny from me!') would pass, and he would soon be readmitted to the family home as well as to the matrimonial bed. Moreover, recognizing a strong basis of sexual jealousy in his wife's anger, he decided it would hasten things along if he were seen with yet another old girlfriend, Kirsten Gille. He knew his wife well. 'Luis, Luis, what am I to do? I want him back. Am I mad or is he mad?' she cried down the phone to Basualdo.

Thierry had not miscalculated his wife's weaknesses and against Basualdo's expected counsel, she took him back. But the short acrimonious parting had not gone unnoticed, and although the reason for it was still not known, the marriage became fair game for the press. As she had always done when found out, Christina attempted to staunch the stories with lies ('my father always told me to fight lies with lies,' she privately explained her favourite tactic when dealing with the media). On 12 June, the day after the uneasy reconciliation at Boislande, the London *Daily Mail* received a telex from Geneva: '*Christina and Thierry Roussel announced today that they are determined to bring a legal action against every newspaper or magazine that would publish false news about their private life and especially the libellous information according to which Mrs Christina Roussel made financial gifts to her husband.*' The newspaper ignored the threat.

On 31 July, just six months after Thierry's daughter was born in Paris, Gaby gave birth to his son in Malmo. With the *chutzpah* that Ari had shrewdly perceived a decade earlier, Thierry flew to Sweden in his wife's Falcon 50 for the baptism of his little Erik Christoffe François. In Paris Christina at first put up a brave front for friends who knew what her husband was up to, but it didn't last and at the final moment she cancelled the August invitations to Skorpios, and to Athina's baptism, to some forty guests. 'She was hurt a lot,' says Basualdo, whom she rang in the middle of the night and offered $60,000 to fly to Malmo to take photographs of Gaby and her son. 'I want to see what my husband's child looks like,' she told him poignantly.

Thierry was not pleased when he discovered that Christina had called off the christening party on Skorpios. It was unfair to make Athina the scapegoat for his peccadillo in Malmo, he argued. The party was hastily rearranged. But Christina was not prepared to settle for 'a marriage for public occasions – like my father's marriage to Jackie. I couldn't bear that kind of sham,' she told friends. 'Thierry and I fight all the time, but we both know the day we stop fighting is the day our marriage is finished.' (Her dilemma, suggested one of her closest friends in Paris, was that 'she despised Roussel in many ways but she also had this sentimental and sexual fixation about him being the father of her child. Athina was Roussel's strength, she was his grip on Christina, the leverage that no other man in the world had on her.')

Although he was not liked by Christina's friends and relations, nor trusted by the 'uncles' in Monte Carlo and New York, Thierry's own admirers insisted that he had always tried to maintain a dignity in a situation where little dignity was possible. His hopes of establishing his own business interests were dealt a blow when his dream of mass-producing a luxury 168-tonne fibreglass yacht (kingsize stateroom, *en suite* bathroom, gold-plated fittings) collapsed in Italy. Christina bought one of the very few models actually built. It cost $3 million; she named it *Athina R* and presented it to Thierry for his thirty-second birthday. (Eighteen months later, after their divorce, he changed its name to *Boukephalas* and sold it to an Englishman named Peter Clowes for $2.5 million; Clowes was indicted for fraud in 1988 after the £180 million collapse of his investment company.)

It was unfortunate for Marina Dodero and her brother Jorge Tchomlekdjoglou that they chose this sensitive time in Christina's marriage to repay the $4 million they had borrowed in 1981. Their father, Stelios, was dying. In the Greek tradition, he wanted to tidy up his affairs in order to be well received in the hereafter. Far from being pleased with the unexpected settlement, Christina was furious. She enjoyed holding the loan over Marina's head – 'as long as it was there, she knew Marina would always come running,' said Basualdo – and suspected that its repayment was a move to extricate the Doderos and the Tchomlekdjoglous from the obligations of friendship. 'I guess Christina is taking out all her frustration in her marriage on the Tchomlekdjoglous,' said a Buenos Aires friend when it was revealed that the heiress was suing Marina and Jorge for $2 million in unpaid interest on the loan. The case continued for six months, first in Buenos Aires, and later in Athens. But when it came to trial, the two old friends met on the courtroom steps. 'They started crying and embracing each other, full of regrets and recantations, and became inseparable again,' said Basualdo. The case was dropped, the interest money never mentioned again.

Meanwhile, the Roussel marriage continued on its faltering, unhappy journey. 'I cannot go on,' Thierry was telling *France-Soir* in Paris one minute, perhaps to improve his public approval ratings after press reports that his family felt he should be paid $50 million in the event of a final split. 'We have not succeeded in coming to an understanding, in being able to live together. I have offered a man's love and given her a child. But I can no longer stand anonymous letters every day, continually being watched over by her bodyguards and the permanent closed-circuit television camera in every room. I don't want to be known as Mr Onassis. It is really too difficult to live with a legend.' One week later they were together again. Yet even when he was insisting that their difficulties were over, he could not stop himself anticipating the end of the marriage: 'The divorce settlement will be dramatic proof of my total lack of interest in my wife's money,' he promised the London *Daily Mail* in the same breath that he had proclaimed their deep new attachment to each other. Unaware of Gaby and her baby, readers (and reporters) of the on-again off-again marriage saga were perplexed. 'The writing is on the wall, only Thierry keeps knocking down the wall,' a Paris pal of the Frenchman summed up the situation.

Not everybody took it so lightly, however. Shortly after Christina's thirty-fifth birthday (and the inevitable grand party at Maxim's), Stavros Niarchos saw her in St Moritz. It was obvious that she was back on the fatal antidepressants, and she looked terrible: unhappy, puffy, without any sort of spark. 'Christina will not live as long as her mother lived. Mark my words,' he told his sons.

—14—

*While your friend holds you
affectionately by both your
hands you are safe, for you can
watch both his*

Ambrose Bierce
The Cynic's Word Book

WHEN HE TALKED ABOUT IT LATER ON , Luis Basualdo made it sound like the act of a Good Samaritan who had been dreadfully misunderstood. But James Blandford remains convinced that he, himself, had been cunningly duped by Basualdo, and was deeply hurt when Christina accused him of stealing her money in league with the glamorous Argentinian. 'I said, "Christina, I have never ripped anyone off in my life. I may have done some bad things but I have never done that,"' the marquess later remembered his passionate denial of what he suspected was a million-dollar scam. Luis still calls it the Landeck misunderstanding, and blames it on the casual nature of his arrangements with Christina.

This is James Blandford's version of what happened in the summer of 1985:

Cured of his heroin addiction after a period in jail for breaking a probation order, he and Basualdo had become buddies. The polo-player was living the life of an English squire in Gloucestershire, hunting with the Duke of Beaufort and other aristocrats. He was also still close to Christina, and still secretly on her payroll. Moreover, she had recently paid him an extra $30,000 to spend a week with her at Avenue Foch while Thierry was in hospital having his appendix removed.

Shortly after this short, rewarding visit, Basualdo and James set out on a tour of Europe in Basualdo's Mercedes. They were heading eventually for Cadaques in Spain, where Basualdo promised to introduce James to Daphne Guinness, an heiress of the brewing dynasty. Basualdo claimed to have had an affair with the beautiful eighteen-year-old blonde in London and confidently predicted a similar experience for James. Certainly it was this pleasant expectation that was uppermost in the marquess's mind on the August morning they left St Moritz to drive across Europe. Perhaps it was because of this that James did not pay too much attention to the unusual events that followed.

'First I have to do a little banking business, my boy,' Basualdo told him before they left St Moritz. He had several times proudly showed the marquess a statement of his Crédit Suisse account with a credit balance of almost 500,000 Swiss francs, and James was not surprised when Basualdo demanded and got a personal appointment with the bank's senior man in St Moritz, the man who dealt with Christina's business, Mr Matisse.

Fifteen minutes later, Basualdo came out of the bank and announced, 'Now we go to Austria. I have some more banking to do.' Still with his mind on Daphne, James was surprised when they arrived in the little town of Lanbeck and Basualdo asked him, 'Which bank should I bank with here, my boy?' James said he had no strong feelings in the matter and Basualdo decided he liked the look of the Bank of Tyrol. 'He gave me the keys of the car and told me to come back in fifteen minutes. I was quite hungry, and went and got a sandwich,' James later recalled.

When he returned to the bank, Basualdo was waiting. 'He said, "Look, my boy, I've told the manager who you are and he says he has never seen a real English aristocrat before and he'd like to meet you." So I went in and Bas introduced us. And something I don't quite understand, he gave my passport to the bank manager.' Believing that the Austrian merely wished to see proof that he truly was who Basualdo claimed him to be, James did not closely follow the conversation between the two men, part of which was conducted in German. 'There was something about a password which you use for the banker johnnies to send you money. Bas told me about this, but wouldn't let on what the password was.'

In the autumn of 1986, Christina received a call from her Monte Carlo office and was informed that her Crédit Suisse account in St Moritz, which usually contained between one and two million dollars, was almost empty. What were her instructions? How could that be? she asked. She had not used the account since February, when it had plenty of money in it. A rapid investigation revealed that over a period of twelve months $1.2 million had been transferred to the account of a

Herr Charles James Spencer at the Bank of Tyrol in Landeck. Christina said that the only Spencer she knew was Charles James Spencer Churchill, the Marquess of Blandford. She could not believe that her former stepbrother had been siphoning money from her account. The bank produced voice recordings – the password was *parakolo*, Greek for 'please' – and Christina immediately identified Basualdo as the mysterious 'Herr Spencer'.

In their separate and distinct ways, few men were closer to her than James and Luis Basualdo, and Christina did not know how to deal with the situation. She was hurt, angry and frustrated. She called Sunbun and told him what had happened. Sunbun immediately called James, who denied everything and expressed profound shock. Christina flew to London to confront James herself. She invited him and his sister Henrietta to dinner at Pier 31, a Chelsea restaurant part-owned by Princess Margaret's son Viscount Linley and the photographer Earl of Lichfield. 'She had a Greek fellow with her, a lawyer. She asked me to tell him exactly what had happened in Lanbeck. He asked me if I had signed anything, that sort of thing. Christina said, "You must have had something to do with it, James."' This is when he told his former stepsister that he may have done some bad things in his life, but he had never ripped anyone off. 'I don't think she believed me. I was very upset.' The dinner continued awkwardly. Driving home, Henrietta told her brother, 'Don't take it to heart, James. She is very, very unhappy. She doesn't know what she's saying.'

Appearing a few days later to accept the marquess's innocence, Christina invited him to lunch at her suite at the Park Lane Hilton. But when he arrived at 1.30 p.m. Eleni told him that Christina was still asleep and did not wish to be wakened. 'Christina later called and said she was sorry and invited me again. Half a dozen times the same thing happened. I'd turn up and she was asleep and not to be disturbed. I gave up finally. It was sad, because I never saw her again,' Blandford would later recall.

Meanwhile, the net was closing in on Luis Basualdo. Two summers earlier he had been stopped at 4 a.m. in one of London's red light districts and arrested on the suspicion of driving while under the influence of alcohol. He spent the night in a cell in Paddington Green police station, and in court later that morning was given unconditional bail for the case to be heard at a later date. But police from that moment on had been unable to track him down, and a warrant was issued for his arrest.

In November 1987, acting on a tip-off, the police arrested him at the Ritz Hotel. He again spent the night at Paddington Green. The following morning at Marlborough Street magistrates' court, he pleaded guilty to the drink-driving offence, was find £200 and banned from driving in Britain for twelve months.

But as he left the court he was detained by detectives and taken to Rochester Row police station, where he was informed that the Austrian police sought him in connection with the Lanbeck affair. Meanwhile, until the extradition papers came through, he must surrender his passport to the British police. He handed over his American passport (he had become a US citizen in 1979) and went back to Clare Lawman's Knightsbridge flat where he had left his clothes, took her out to dinner and, the following morning, left the country on his Argentinian passport.

It was not until this moment, according to Basualdo's own later account of events, that he had any idea that he was a wanted man and that Christina had made a statement to the Austrian police implicating him in what appeared to be a massive fraud. He was furious, he claimed. For he was sure that Christina had authorized the Lanbeck account herself!

This is Luis Basualdo's version of what happened in the summer of 1985:

'My situation with Christina was that she always said that she would give me ten times my salary if ever she found someone else. When she married Roussel she wanted to keep her promise, she gave me a little bit here, a little bit there. But she said, "I don't want Thierry to find out, I don't want the bank to find out I give you so much money, so why don't you open an account in another country, a secret account, and we can use that to pay the doctor in New York [who supplied her with her 'black beauties'], and Blandford and all those other bills?" She reckoned she owed more or less a million.

'She wanted to help Blandford out because he was desperate, a drug addict. He used to come to the Ritz Hotel at three in the morning begging me for money, crying. I just couldn't put up with this and said to Christina, "You almost locked him up in a loony bin, you help." So she said I was to get James to open an account. She suggested Austria, so Blandford and I went to Lanbeck, the closest place to Switzerland. The account was opened by Charles James Spencer Churchill, Marquess of Blandford. The passport on the front says Marquess of Blandford.

Inside it says Charles James Spencer Churchill. They settled on Charles James Spencer because they were trying to be accommodating. The account was to receive money from Christina's account. The money was transferred by cheque or by wire. They were absolutely genuine cheques. The amount was over $1.2 million. Some money had to go to the doctor in New York. Blandford received about $60,000.

'Blandford opened the account in his name with his passport. It was exactly what Christina wanted. But then she tried to cover her tracks. She was afraid of Thierry, annoyed with me because I hadn't gone back to Sweden to try to get pictures of Gaby and the baby; I hadn't paid the doctor in New York some money I was supposed to have paid him . . . so she denounced me.'

Safely back in Buenos Aires, Basualdo called Christina in Paris and demanded an explanation. Remarkably, she advised him to forget all about it. 'Forget it!' he remembers retorting angrily. 'I organized the whole thing just as you wanted it, so that I could give money to people like James and the doctor in New York who sends you the *mavro mavros*, and you try to have me put in prison!' Thanks to her, he said, he was now on the lam. Again, she told him to forget about it. 'She said, "Luis, I'm dropping all charges. I was very upset. You didn't pay the people you were meant to pay, you didn't get the pictures I wanted. I know you're not guilty. There is no more problem. You don't have to worry about a thing."'

By this time Christina had another major problem on her mind, and a million-dollar misunderstanding, or scam ('What's a million dollars to Christina? A week's tax-free income, give or take a hundred thou,' said an Onassis staffer in Monte Carlo who had followed the Lanbeck affair in growing disbelief), was last week's news. The new problem was really part of an old problem that she knew was never going to go away: Gaby was again pregnant by Thierry. It was the last straw.

Things had been tense between them since December, when Christina began talking openly about the millions (some reports claimed $57 million) she had given her husband since their marriage. One evening at The Club, the St Moritz discothèque Peppo Vannini had opened in the Chesa Veglia after leaving the King's Club, the affectionate and headstrong Constantine Niarchos noticed that his cousin was being ignored by her husband. He asked her to dance. She looked at Thierry,

and said no. 'I said, "Well, it certainly won't cost you $10 million!"
Thierry got up and from the back punched me four or five times. I
turned round and threw a kick at him,' Constantine later recalled the
incident.

'From that moment, those who knew Christina best were saying that
it could be only a matter of months before she gave Thierry the heave-
ho,' said an English acquaintance who had witnessed the unseemly
fracas. In the New Year, Roussel left on an extended business trip to
Texas, and when he returned in May 1987 he had a new daughter –
Sandrine Johanna Hélène Francine, born in Dallas and registered
'Roussel Landhage' – and an ex-wife on his hands.

As in the past, a divorce to Christina was not meant to spoil a perfectly
good relationship. 'Divorce was just something I had to do for the sake
of my pride,' she told Florence Grinda. But almost as soon as the ink
was dry on the decree *nisi*, she became obsessed with the idea of winning
Thierry back again. She was encouraged when he rented a house close
to Boislande so that he could spend time with both families. She tried
to make him jealous by setting her cap at Frederick Bauche, the son of
Henri Roussel's mistress, Marcelline (Henri and Marcelline had moved
into the fifth floor of Avenue Foch), and a man deeply disliked by
Thierry. For a short while, it looked as if her pursuit might evolve into
something serious. She even told Florence that she hoped that Frederick
would father her a child. But when Frederick, whose marriage was
anyway under strain (it later ended in divorce), told Christina he was
leaving his wife, Christina called it a day. 'I got cold feet,' she confessed
to Florence, although some who knew of her scheme and the reason for
it believed that 'Christina accepted that Thierry was not the jealous
type.'

Deprived not for the first time in her affairs of the jealousy weapon,
Christina tried a different approach. She made friends with Gaby, and
her children. Shortly after dispatching gifts to the baby's christening in
October, she invited the mother and child to Boislande for tea. With
Thierry hovering nervously, the first meeting between the two women
with nothing and everything in common was a delicate moment. And
whatever they felt and thought as women, as mothers they rejoiced to
see Athina and her half-brother Erik getting on so well together. And
the sight of the new Roussel baby started Christina on a round of visits
to the best gynaecologists in Paris and London. 'Thierry, I want, I must

have, another child, and only you can be its father,' she was telling him by Christmas. They were still lovers, she made no secret of it. But the drugs, the violent swings in her body weight, her unhealthy diet and lifestyle, had all taken a toll. Twice in the following six months she confided to friends that she was pregnant; both times she miscarried early. 'To have another child became an obsession with her,' said Florence Grinda. After a profound but mercifully shortlived depression following her second miscarriage, she suddenly brightened up. 'We have a plan now. It's going to be fine,' she announced confidently and mysteriously. But she would not say what the plan was. Friends guessed that she intended next time she got pregnant to take to her bed for nine months, as she had with Athina.

Instead of her summer sojourn on Skorpios, Christina rented Le Trianon in St Jean-Cap Ferrat for the months of July and August. It was a magnificent villa in its own secluded grounds, with a pool and tennis court. Only compared to the luxuries of Skorpios was it nothing to write home about. But its advantages from Thierry's point of view were immeasurable. The Côte d'Azur was his neck of the woods. His mother's family were considerable property owners in Nice (including the Westminster Hotel) and he had spent his youth in the clubs and restaurants of the Riviera. He had never conquered Skorpios, where despite his best efforts he continued to be known as Mr Onassis. And when the Greek police discovered Christina's name at the top of a terrorist hit list, he used the threat to relocate his ex-wife and child to France. In France he had more control over the guest list too. And ever-accommodating, Christina had also rented the villa next to Le Trianon for Gaby and her children. 'There is no shame in admitting one loves two women,' Thierry proclaimed his Gallic *modus operandi*. 'Christina and Gaby have become good friends and they want the children to grow up together. They see each other often and when they don't they write to each other.'

But when they went partying to the high-society watering-holes – the Falcon and the helicopter were kept busy throughout the summer – Gaby was often noticeably absent. She was excluded from a jaunt to Capri in July, and it was a white-gowned, radiant-looking Christina who clung to Thierry's arm at the famous Red Cross Ball in Monte Carlo in August. In August too she invited two hundred of her favourite people to a party at Le Trianon – and had the napkins inscribed *Christina and Thierry.* 'They are so in love,' said Anne Lyon, one of the many guests who believed they would soon be celebrating a second-time-around marriage.

But in September Christina returned alone to Paris while Thierry took her jet back to Sweden, where he had bought Gaby and her children a house on a peninsula on the outskirts of Gothenberg.

But Christina was happy. She had her plan.

—15—

*I am Alpha and Omega, the
beginning and the ending,
Saith the Lord*

The Revelations of St John the Divine 1.8

FATE EXISTS, CHRISTINA HAD TOLD A FRIEND a week before in Paris when asked why she wanted to buy a home in Argentina. On the threshold of a new beginning, she was sure of the happiness the future held in store for her. 'A new page, Thierry, a *new* start,' she told Roussel, who had expressed his doubts about a place so far away, and perhaps beyond his sway. But this time even Roussel's disapproval could not deter Christina. Buenos Aires had everything she needed and adored – rich friends who loved her, beautiful men who wanted to love her, wonderful stores, sunshine and nightlife.

She arrived on 9 November, a Wednesday. Officially staying with Marina and Alberto 'Dode' Dodero, she also took a sixth-floor room at the Alvear Palace, and a further room for Eleni next to hers. Her room at the hotel was to be her office, from which she could organize her search for the new home; it would also enable her to telephone her friends in Europe and the United States, and chat for as long as she wanted, an addiction that she knew could make even the most understanding hosts nervous.

'I feel good here,' Christina told Mercedes Zavalia, adding that she planned an extended stay – 'until I find what I really want'. she was looking at premises on several of the fashionable avenues, including a $4.2 million penthouse on Recoleta. She was also contemplating a 'family-size' *estancia* in the pampas. 'I want Athina to have a proper childhood, to grow up in a proper family atmosphere,' she said with touching earnestness, as if still tormented and still haunted by her own alienated childhood.

Christina had planned to bring her daughter with her but at the last moment it was discovered that she had an infection of the middle ear (*otitis media*, sometimes caused in small children by leaping into a pool without holding their nose). It was decided that Athina should follow in a few weeks, when the problem had yielded to antibiotics.

Christina genuinely missed her daughter. She had strong parental emotions, and had made plans to explore the city with Athina, to discover its secrets and its pleasures together. One idea was to trace her own father's footsteps in Buenos Aires. She had drawn up a list of the places he had known – the Teatro Colón, for example, where he had seen his first opera, *La Bohème* (and seduced his first famous lady, the Italian soprano Claudia Muzio).

Mercedes Zavalia, who had given Christina the street-maps to pinpoint Ari's travels through the city sixty-five years before, said: 'It wasn't simply nostalgia, I am sure of that. It was important to her. I don't know what she expected to discover. Maybe some shocks of recognition. Maybe some truth about herself.'

According to another close source, Christina was drawn to Buenos Aires because it was where she believed she would find 'her own place, and her daughter's place, in the Onassis epos'.

Christina's sense of a new beginning did not mean that she intended to abandon *all* her old ways. This was the pleasure season in Buenos Aires, the time for entertaining, before the fierce summer heat dried up the land and sapped the energy of its people. The Doderos, who had lined up properties for her to see in the day, arranged plenty of parties for the evenings and the long weekends at the Tortugas Country Club.

It was also noticeable that the Doderos' relationship with Christina since the night of Marina's fortieth birthday bash at Le Club had moved into a new and fascinating mode. Encouraged or perhaps inspired by the rumours that had been lighted that night at Le Club, Marina had become profoundly and increasingly taken with the notion that her spiritual 'little sister' might also soon become her incarnate little sister-in-law.

Certainly there was a tangible air of anticipation at the dinner parties the Doderos gave at home for Christina. Placed beside her, Jorge Tchomlekdjoglou basked in his new reputation as a ladies' man. 'He positively bloomed,' said a friend who had known Jorge for thirty years and had never seen him bloom for a lady before. 'It was a whole new ball game.'

The idea of having a new man to go with her new start was not unattractive to Christina, and she did nothing to quieten the rumours nor to discourage the matchmaking dreams of the Doderos. And, anyway, she was genuinely quite fond of Jorge. Jorge was comfortable. Jorge was sweet. Above all, Jorge Tchomlekdjoglou was *controllable*, she confided to girlfriends she was calling in London and Paris, and who were now reading in magazines and gossip columns stories of her new lover with the unpronounceable name.

Among those friends she was telephoning daily was Dominique Rizzo, wife of Paris furniture designer and photographer Willy Rizzo. In the final months of her second pregnancy, Dominique had had to decline Christina's invitation to accompany her on the trip to Argentina, and she was now keen to know *exactly* what was going on in her absence.

'Have you slept with Jorge?' she asked with the candour that Christina expected and always returned in friendship.

'Maybe I made love to him ... once,' Christina replied with an air of uncertainty unusual in such matters.

It did not, thought Dominique, 'sound like an experience Christina would never forget'.

Although she paid an agency to collect and send her everything printed about her anywhere in the world, Christina began urging friends to fax the stories and items about her and Jorge appearing in the papers and magazines in Europe. The stories usually ensured she was the focus of attention at dinner parties or at lunches with the girls. 'If she was represented in a bad light,' said one Paris girlfriend, 'she would pretend to be angry and upset and complain of its distortions. But she enjoyed the limelight the stories gave her. She never sued *anybody* for libel *ever*.'

According to one reliable source in Buenos Aires, Christina's unusually keen interest in the Jorge-and-Christina stories was quite another matter. 'She wanted the rumours to irritate Roussel. She wanted the stories to provoke him into some sort of response. She wanted him to believe that Jorge was some kind of threat, a serious stud. That's why she played along with the Doderos. That's the *only* reason she sat still for all that nonsense about brother Jorge. She was using the Doderos just as much as socially they thought they were using her.'

Thierry Roussel continued to rest securely at the centre of her universe. They continued to be occasional lovers, the last occasion being Christina's visit to Boislande, when they had again discussed the possibility of Roussel fathering another child for Christina. According to one despairing Onassis source, she had promised to pay Thierry $10 million on delivery, 'and nothing in the world could disabuse her of the idea that it would be ten mil well spent'.

But he made no secret of the fact that he was not easily aroused by his former wife. (He loved her, he insisted, but that was not the same thing at all.) And since the opportunities when they could be together were limited by time and space, if not seemliness, and might not always be cyclically propitious, Christina had suggested that he supply her with a sperm bank on which she could make demands on the most auspicious days in the month. Roussel agreed, and duly collected a $160,000 Ferrari Testarossa from a grateful and ever-loving Christina.

And so it was that each month on the day her cycle suggested she was most likely to conceive, her gynaecologist implanted Roussel's semen in her.

This was her 'plan', the plan she had been hugging to herself since the summer in St Jean-Cap Ferrat, the plan whose successful fruition would prove to the whole world that Thierry Roussel was still hers, if not quite hers alone.

Meanwhile, in Buenos Aires the eventful round of house-hunting by day and partying at night continued. She quickly worked out her own list of favourite places. La Biela and the neighbouring Café de la Paix were high on the list, also Au Fin Bec (the best French restaurant in town), La Casona de Reque (Italian), and Cabaña, famous for its T-bone steaks. The nightclubs she liked best were Mau Mau, Hippopotamus and Le Club. All these names were carefully noted in her Filofax, to which she attached almost talismanic significance since her father had bequeathed her his notebooks and inculcated in her, as his father had in him, the need to 'make a note of everything'.

On successive evenings she attended a reception at the American Embassy (posing in a short red dress for *Gente* magazine), and a party at the Uruguayan Embassy, at which she wore her $2 million diamond drop, and stylishly ignored the fact that Jorge, in a lounge suit, was the only man in the room not wearing a tuxedo. She appeared to be in tremendous form.

On 17 November, she dined at the Cabaña with Jorge and the

Doderos. She talked elliptically about her recent trip to Europe. 'I made some business, and I solved some family problems,' she said, repeating more or less what she had told the Greek Archbishop Ganadius Chrisolakis, with whom she had lunched the previous day. It was noticeable that some of the previous evenings' bounce had gone out of her. She did not want to go on to a club and they returned to the Doderos' apartment on Callao, where they continued to talk and play music for several hours. Although Christina had a bedroom and her own private bathroom in the Doderos' twelve-room apartment, she never spent the night there, and at around 4 a.m. she kissed the Doderos goodnight and returned to the hotel.

Christina did not stay long in the Alvear Palace. At about 5 a.m., barefoot, wearing a Walkman to which she was listening intently, she walked out of the hotel. Ignoring the concierge's warnings about going out alone at that hour, and paying no attention to his anxious offer to get her a cab, she turned right up Avenida Alvear and kept going.

She returned at 8 a.m., still without shoes, still wearing the Walkman. Telling the operator that she did not want any calls until further notice, she slept probably until midday, when she summoned Eleni. She complained of feeling cold; the noonday temperature was in the seventies. Eleni packed extra sweaters and jackets for the weekend at Tortugas.

Waiting for the limousine to arrive, Christina again complained of feeling cold, and began to shiver. Marina Dodero wanted to call a doctor; Christina wouldn't hear of it. 'It's nothing serious, maybe a slight chill,' she insisted. After a little while, the shivering stopped and Christina appeared to recover.

The ride out to Tortugas ahead of the evening traffic was quietly cheerful with talk of the weekend ahead: the parties, the barbecue arranged for that evening, who was going to be there, who was not. Their voices ran on pleasantly. As usual, Christina would be the star. She knew it. The Doderos knew it. She was still their *La Reina*, the Queen.

Arriving at the club it was discovered that its unreliable telephone system had broken down, and would probably remain down for the weekend. Christina went to the telephone exchange in the village to call Athina. They talked and talked, even though Christina had to take the call standing up in a public booth. They discussed Athina's coming visit to Argentina. Christina told her she was going to love the big country. 'It's wonderful here,' she said. 'We shall buy a huge ranch and you will have your own pony.' She explained the problems with the telephone at the club and promised to call Athina again on Monday.

The call, as Eleni knew it would, put Christina in an altogether better mood. In the evening, she took her customary scalding bath, and came out pink as a baby; she spent longer than usual putting on her makeup, which Eleni knew was always a good sign. At the barbecue, both Marina and Alberto said how much better she was looking.

But later in the evening, Christina again began complaining of the cold. She moved closer to the fire, and Eleni fetched her a heavier sweater. It was a spring night, but not cold; in a few weeks the nights would be warm and tacky. Perhaps, Christina said, she had caught a bug. She mentioned her foray the previous early morning, without explaining why she had gone off like that, or saying where she had gone. She continued to be in a happy mood, drinking Coke after Coke. 'She seemed like a very ordinary sort of girl, a girl without a real worry in the world,' thought one guest at the barbecue that night.

At the end of the evening she went for a stroll around the grounds with Jorge, who had his own villa in the grounds, just behind his sister's and Dode's. She really did like him. She liked the way he didn't come at her with all that male aggression; he never pushed her, she had told her girlfriends in Paris. She liked the way he just smiled, and waited. She felt good with him, she told him when she kissed him goodnight.

Kissing the Doderos goodnight at about 1.30 – early for her – Christina said she would be up at nine o'clock. She invited them to join her for a swim after breakfast.

'Goodnight, *Reina*, sleep well and get better,' said Marina.

———

At Tortugas, as nowhere else, Christina liked to rise early, sometimes as early as 8.30. So when, at ten o'clock that fine spring Saturday morning, the Doderos finished their breakfast, Marina went in search of their houseguest.

Summoned by Marina's sudden and terrible screams, Dode, quickly followed by Eleni, raced to the villa.

They found Christina lying naked in a half-filled bath.

It was clear, at least to Eleni, who also noticed with her quick professional eye that the bed had not been slept in, her mistress was dead. Only at the Doderos' did she not wait up for her mistress (Christina insisted), and now the maid who had been nearly a mother to the dead heiress saw with brimming eyes her baby's clothes still on the floor, left where they fell, as Christina had undressed hurriedly, carelessly, as she always did, sure that Eleni would be behind her to pick them up.

What happened next happened quickly, and would become the subject of much talk and speculation in the weeks and months to come.

The Doderos, in a mutual state of shock, ran from the villa calling for a doctor and an ambulance. Dr Arturo Granadillos Fuentes was the first professional man to arrive on the scene. He found the heiress on the bed, her hair still wet. When he attempted to enter the bathroom, where the body had been found, and where he knew there might be evidence to show how she might have died, Dode ordered him out. It was now perfectly clear to everybody that Christina was beyond anyone's help. But Dr Fuentes refused to sign the death certificate, feeling that there were grounds for an autopsy. (Later he would claim he had been refused permission to examine the body thoroughly, and was told to leave the villa 'for asking questions'.)

The body was taken first to a local clinic (the Miraculous Virgin), and shortly afterwards transferred to the exclusive Clinica del Sol in Buenos Aires, whose director, Dr Hernan Bunge, had been among the guests at the previous night's barbecue. In emergency room 201, two examining physicians could only conclude that 'death had occurred some hours before she had been put into the ambulance'; and that her body weight at the time of death was 76 kg (167 pounds). Again the issue of a death certificate was withheld pending an autopsy, and at noon that day Judge Juan Carlos Cardinali was officially notified of a 'doubtful' death. At three o'clock on Saturday afternoon, he signed an order for an autopsy. The news of the death of the most famous heiress in the world was officially out.

Thierry Roussel arrived in Buenos Aires at 11.30 on Sunday morning. He was accompanied by Paul Ionnadis, a close and longtime friend of the Onassis family, and one of the four wise Greeks on Athina's board of trustees (he would inherit $2 million in Christina's will). The thirteen-hour flight from Geneva, the mob of reporters and photographers that had met him at the airport and was now camped outside the Alvear Palace, had destroyed any stoicism Roussel might have shown after hearing the tragic news. He broke down as soon as he stepped into his suite. 'I put my arms around him and held him for a long time,' said Mercedes Zavalia, convinced of his grief, as some were not. 'He sobbed and sobbed.' He was distressed by the rumours that Christina had committed suicide. He had talked to her only the day before and she was full of plans for the future – describing the properties she had seen, wondering where to spend her thirty-eighth birthday on 11 December. Was that the talk of a woman contemplating killing herself? It was the question he asked over and over.

Speculation was running wild and was not calmed by a statement from a federal judge whose district included the Clinica del Sol, claiming that Christina had died 'under questionable circumstances'. Judge Daniel Pitti, in charge of a separate investigation into whether Christina had taken pills shortly before her death, announced that her body could not be removed from the country without judicial permission. It was the stuff of headlines and the darkest rumours. (In France, Jean-Noël Grinda, Roussel's uncle, Athina's godfather and Christina's friend, was sure he knew *exactly* why she had died: he blamed the trauma of the spermatozoa implant surgery Christina had been undergoing every month. 'Her determination to have another child with Thierry killed her,' he said flatly.)

On Monday, Judge Cardinali issued a further statement: the cause of death had been acute pulmonary oedema. It was a condition that can precipitate a heart attack, a spokesman added without actually confirming that she had also suffered a fatal coronary. (The coroner's report also noted that she had not engaged in sexual intercourse in the twenty-four hours prior to her demise.) It was precisely the way her mother had died in Paris fourteen years before. Even the confusion and rumours were the same.

Christina's body, minus its stomach and a number of other organs and tissues which were undergoing forensic tests to establish the quantity and chemical content of the drugs she was now believed to have taken shortly before her death, was driven first to a funeral home, where she was embalmed, and her face made up with her own cosmetics fetched from the hotel. Later that afternoon, the body was laid to rest in an open, white-linen-draped dark wooden casket, with a red rose in her hand, before the altar of the church for the Orthodox archdiocese, where one week earlier she had kneeled and prayed with Archbishop

Chrisolakis for the souls of her mother, father and brother Alexander.

Thierry Roussel waited until dark before he came to the church. For almost an hour he sat alone with the body of the woman he had known for sixteen years, who had loved him so much, whose heart was incurably romantic, foolish, loving and kind, and who had changed his life irrevocably. He was still sobbing when he kissed her goodbye.

The following morning, after Eleni had made a statement detailing the purpose (therapeutic) and the sources (Christina's Paris and New York physicians) of the drugs found at the villa, and in Christina's room at the hotel, Christina's body was released by the Argentine authorities.

On Wednesday, 23 November, accompanied by Roussel, Paul Ionnadis, the Doderos and Jorge, and watched over by her beloved Eleni, Christina Onassis's remains returned to Greece.

—16—

It might make one in love with death,
to think
That one should be buried in so sweet
a place

Percy Bysshe Shelley
Adonais (Preface)

IT RAINED FOREVER THAT FRIDAY, the day of her funeral, a torrential
rain that would not relent. Mourners got wet through in the few yards
they had to run between the Grand Bretagne Hotel and the black
Mercedes limousines lined up to take them to the Fotini Cathedral; and
they were drenched again dashing between cars and church, fighting
their way through jostling crowds (who had been gathering in the
downpour since early morning) who had come to watch and remember
the last great Onassis show the world would ever see.

Inside the cathedral, bright with klieg lights and burning candles, the
sound of a thousand cameras accompanied the choir. (More than a
hundred journalists had been accredited by the Onassis organization to
cover the service.) Scuffles broke out, chairs were overturned as reporters
competed with photographers for the best views. 'This is mayhem, this
is dreadful,' said the Duke of Marlborough with sadness in his voice
for the little girl who used to call him Sunbun.

'It was horrendous,' James Blandford said later about that Friday.
'We stayed at the Grand Bretagne. Thierry was there with his lot and
we had dinner there and they didn't want to speak to us. It was them
and us, it was all very strained. And the cathedral was a bloody circus
... up all those steps, everyone was jostling, pushing and shouting,
wailing, gnashing. Knowing Christina, what she would have wanted
was a little family funeral on Skorpios, to put her down without all the
nonsense ... put her to bed and let the waves of the Ionian do the rest.
We left after the cathedral service. I would have liked to have gone to
Skorpios, but no one asked us.'

Outside the cathedral fans were beginning to loot flowers for souvenirs from the wreaths stacked against the church doors and carpeting the steps. Crosses of chrysanthemums and daisies were stripped down to the bare wire. When Thierry Roussel appeared walking behind the coffin, some people in the crowd called out 'Assassin, assassin' (not understanding Greek, he supposed they were words of commiseration and answered with the small sad smile of the bereaved); but some women also tried to tear at his clothes and run their fingers through his long blond hair, which fell over his collar as if he were a pop idol.

———

There were no crowds on Skorpios.

Less than forty people followed Christina's walnut coffin (made, as her father's had been made, from one of the island's trees) through the wind and dust up the hill to the tiny chapel, where her father and her brother were buried side by side.

The mourners knew – it was part of their grief – that the simple service was not only for Christina, the last Onassis, but for Skorpios too.

The tiny Onassis kingdom had lasted exactly twenty-five years. The famous and the infamous, the rich and the fashionable of that quarter of the twentieth century had been spoiled and scandalized, enchanted and seduced on what Ari had once called his 'wild little rock' in the Ionian Sea.

It was where Maria Callas's heart was filled with hope, then broken.

And where Jacqueline Bouvier Kennedy became the second Mrs Onassis.

It was where Ari buried his son, and his future.

Now it was history.

The large dining room was lit by candles, the way Christina liked it best. The mourners were offered the finest food and the finest wines. They talked quietly and told their strongest memories of Christina, and the yacht named after her (which she had bequeathed to the Greek government), and happier days on Skorpios. Some smiled and some laughed; a few sobbed silently.

But November was not the season for Skorpios. November was Paris, London and New York. And these were people who followed the seasons as closely as housemartins follow the sun. And less than two hours after they had come, the helicopters began taking back to Actium those who had known Christina best. Uncle George Livanos. Her Niarchos cousins, Philippe, Constantine and Maria (but not their father, Stavros). Aunt Kaliroi. Paul Ionnadis. Eleni Syros. Former husbands Alexander Andreadis and Thierry Roussel, but not the Russian and not Joe Bolker, who had died two years before. From Actium the Lears and the Falcons would fly them back to London, to Paris, to Geneva, as they had done in all the fine summers when Christina was *La Reina*.

Index